APPROACHES TO MODERN
JUDAISM

Program in Judaic Studies
Brown University
BROWN JUDAIC STUDIES
Edited by

Jacob Neusner,
Wendell S. Dietrich, Ernest S. Frerichs,
Alan Zuckerman

Number 49

APPROACHES TO MODERN
JUDAISM

edited by
Marc Lee Raphael

APPROACHES TO MODERN JUDAISM

edited by
Marc Lee Raphael

Scholars Press
Chico, California

APPROACHES TO MODERN JUDAISM

edited by
Marc Lee Raphael

Library of Congress Cataloging in Publication Data
Main entry under title:
Approaches to modern Judaism.

(Brown Judaic studies ; no. 49)
Includes bibliographical references and index.
Contents: Love, marriage, and the modernization of the
Jews / David Biale — Secular religiosity / Paul Mendes-
Flohr — Judaism and Marxism / Michael Dobkowski —
[etc.]
1. Judaism—History—Modern period, 1750- —
Addresses, essays, lectures. 2. Judaism—United States—
Addresses, essays, lectures. I. Raphael, Marc Lee.
II. Series.
BM195.A66 1983   296   83-14202
ISBN 0-89130-647-1

Printed in the United States of America

For Mel and Doc

exemplars of modern Judaism

TABLE OF CONTENTS

The idea for APPROACHES TO MODERN JUDAISM came from Professor Jacob Neusner of Brown University who hoped that such a volume would serve as a vehicle in three ways. First, it would enable colleagues to address methodological issues in various fields of modern Judaic Studies, especially by asking questions such as what is the most pressing issue in a given area? what have been the traditional ways of looking at these problems? and what might constitute a new approach? It might also stimulate, in various fields, non-methodological articles of substance. Finally, this series might generate fresh thinking about what constitutes modernity, and a discussion about the relationship between Judaism and various elements of modernity.

David Biale explores premodern and modern Jewish marriages in his search for Jewish attitudes and norms which serve as indices of modernity, noting the modern elements, influences and "style" within the traditional institution of marriage and its process of modernization.

Paul Mendes-Flohr argues that secularization is a salient feature of modernity, introduces us to the phrase "secular religiosity" with confidence that it is inherent in the individuation of society and culture that characterizes modernity, and explores post-traditional or modern Jewish sensibilities.

Michael Dobkowski bemoans a lack of interest among Judaic scholars in Marxist theory, and in urging a dialogue between Judaism and Marxist thought he explores several Jewish responses to modernism and suggests ways in which these modern responses have been linked to traditional Judaism.

David Ellenson explores the impact of modernity upon the Orthodox Jewish community of nineteenth century Germany, and especially the response of Rabbi Esriel Hildesheimer to the problem of religious authority. Using categories drawn from the sociology of religion, Ellenson explores Hildesheimer's responses to the challenges of modernity, clarifies the oft-used but vaguely defined phrase "Modern Orthodox" and Hildesheimer's pivotal role in its formulation, reflects upon the modern vs. sectarian orthodox struggles in Germany a century ago, and reveals how modernism (values of Western culture) and tradition (Modern Orthodox) may coexist in one man.

Through a comparison of the literary expression of Southerners and Jews, Stephen J. Whitfield writes about the distinguishing characteristics of the American Jewish experience. These features--set aganst the background of modernity--include the Jewish historical consciousness, emphasis upon family, special contribution to modern culture, and unique sensibilities.

B. Barry Levy argues that the intellectual and ideological commitments of any Jewish group may be judged by the ways in which it interprets the Bible, and that contemporary Orthodox Jews--who produce, support and study the Artscroll Bible Commentaries--are no exception. He examines, as a "modern" reader, this new commentary, and enables us to evaluate several dimensions of this contemporary Jewish community: the way it believes the Bible should be taught and preached and the ways in which it has understood--and misunderstood--its rich Jewish heritage of Bible-related literature and the contemporary world of Bible study.

These volumes, of which this is the first, will appear as often as necessary. I am extremely grateful to the Ohio State University College of Humanities for providing the typing support and to Professor Jacob Neusner for making publication possible.

Marc Lee Raphael
June, 1983

LOVE, MARRIAGE AND THE MODERNIZATION OF THE JEWS

David Biale
Suny Binghamton

In the early 1760s, Moses Mendelssohn wrote to his fiancée, Fromet Guggenheim: "Your amourousness requires me in these letters to transcend all conventional ceremonies. For, just as we needed no marriage brokers for our (engagement), so we need no ceremonies for our correspondence . . . The heart will answer these instead." And in another place: "Even the kisses that I stole from your lips were mixed with some bitterness, for the approaching separation made me heavy of heart and incapable of enjoying a pure pleasure."[1] In his classic article from 1945, Jacob Katz argued that with these letters, Mendelssohn marked the end of traditional Jewish norms of betrothal and marriage and the beginnings of romantic love and free choice.[2] Katz thus anticipated by nearly three decades the arguments of what is sometimes called the "sentiments school" of family history.[3] Historians like Edward Shorter and Lawrence Stone have asserted that traditional marriage was an instrumental relationship characterized by a low level of affection.[4] In the eighteenth century, a revolution of romantic sentiment turned marriage into a relationship of companionship and affection and thus contrubuted to the development of the modern nuclear family. Shorter attributed this change to the impact of industrialization on the working class while Stone, coming closer to Katz's argument about the Jews, saw it as a result of the rise of individualism among the upper and middle classes.

The sentiments school has been attacked on a variety of grounds which need not detain us here.[5] The relationship of family history to the other indices of modernization remains very much an open question. What may the particular history of the Jews contribute to this discussion? A common argument holds that the Jews, as a relatively urbanized people, were more prepared for modern society than were the peasant populations of Western and Eastern Europe. A study of Latvian Jews suggests that the family structure of eighteenth century Jews more closely resembled the modern nuclear family than did the extended family perhaps more common to medieval peasant society.[6] But Katz's work argues that even if Jewish family structure was closer to a modern model, Jewish attitudes and norms were anything but modern until the new values of the European enlightenment infiltrated the Jewish community from the outside. For Katz, "modernization" of Jewish marital attitudes resulted from a backward people's imitation of the European revolution.

Against Katz, Azriel Shochat argued that, at least in Central Europe, a shift in values occurred within the Jewish community as early as the late seventeenth century, thus predating Mendelssohn by one or two generations.[7] Shochat focused on deviations from rabbinic norms and concluded that the Jewish enlightenment was the later product of an earlier social transformation. As the power of the rabbis and the traditional community declined following the Thirty Years War, new values, including new marital values, became widely accepted. Shochat did not identify the origins of these values but implied that they were influenced by non-Jewish ideas to which the Jews were now more receptive. Katz's reply to Shochat was that all societies include exceptions and deviations from the norms, but that the exceptions did not indicate the triumph of new norms: they still believed in traditional values even if they rebelled against them. Only Mendelssohn and his generation fully adopted a new system of values.[8]

In contrast to both Katz and Shochat, I should like to propose a new framework in which to evaluate exceptions. Exceptional behavior was neither meaningless, as Katz implies, nor the harbinger of new values, as Shocat does. Instead, the exceptions indicate that early modern Jewish society offered a wider range of possibilities than the official literature (rabbinic codes, etc) admits. In addition, some exceptional behavior reflected values shared by the society as a whole, but which found expression in socially unconventional ways. For instance, rather than assuming that arranged marriages were devoid of sentiment and built on cold calculation, we should imagine a society that expected the arranged marriage to be accompanied by love. Those who rebelled against parental authority did not espouse different values from their parents, but rejected the specific choices offered to them. Such rebels were not representative, but they do testify that the possibilities for romantic sentiment were much greater than we imagine today. Their example also suggests that the "modernization" of marital values among the Ashkenazic Jews did not follow the model of linear "progress" proposed by Shorter and Stone for France and England or Katz for the Jews.

We shall have to consult materials from the responsa and sermonic literature in order to develop our case. Jewish historians have long recognized the problems of dealing with these kind of texts. The responsa literature, like any court cases, is bound to be anecdotal and not always representative, while sermons often exaggerate certain tendencies and present them as more widespread than they actually are. These materials can often be most productively used if one can find social comments en passant, that is, as incidental to the main issue, which is more likely to be distorted for polemical or legal purposes. In any event, my purpose in using these texts is not to make generalizations about what everyone experienced but to discover what was possible within the norms of traditional Jewish society.

The major issue of contention here will be whether love was part of the norms associated with marriage. As in any society, some people experience love while others do not. It would be exceedingly difficult to determine (as some sentiments historians have tried) whether the percentage of people who experienced such emotions was fewer or greater in one period than in another. My goal instead is to discover whether love was part of the normative system that would be inculcated in young people as they approached the age of marriage, not whether they actually felt it or not.

Love in Premodern Marriages

The word "love" will present us with serious problems of definition. What love meant to the Romantics of the early nineteenth century was quite different from what it means today and, similarly, what it might have meant in Ashkenazic society (the relatively unitary Jewish culture of Central and Eastern Europe up until the eighteenth century and continuing into the nineteenth century in the East). What love might mean to a pubescent boy in one culture might be quite different from what it would mean to a twenty-five year-old independent man in the same culture. I would immediately want to distinguish between the companionship or affection referred to in the law codes as an important reason for marriage and love. The kind of affection which may develop between man and wife may or may not be preceded by romantic attraction, but it is a result of day-to-day living together. What we are dealing with here are the emotions experienced by people before marriage or in the first flush of married life. These feelings may or may not have had an erotic component, although some of the evidence we shall see suggests that for engaged couples, love and erotic attraction were believed to be connected.

Neither the law codes nor the marriage manuals in our possession refer explicitly to love and we must search elsewhere for it. Certainly, the norms of society are not to be found only in law codes and, in fact, many norms may never be written down in prescriptive texts. One unusual text which repeatedly discusses love both prior to and outside of marriage is the twelfth century Sefer Hasidim.[9] The author clearly has in mind something quite different from affection that develops within a marriage, for, in one case, he specifically refers to a man's love for a woman he does not even know.

The Sefer Hasidim comes from a period much earlier than that which is our focus here: the seventeenth, eighteenth and early nineteenth centuries. But in this later period, we also find evidence that once a marriage was arranged according to the standard criteria of lineage, learning and wealth, romantic feelings not only sometimes developed of their own accord (as Katz was willing to admit) but they were expected to develop. For instance, Abraham Ber Gottlober, the early nineteenth century maskil, who was certainly no admirer of traditional marriage, relates that he began to develop feelings of love for his bride-to-be even before he met her.[10] Now, we have no way of knowing just what Gottlober meant by love and since his memoir was composed many years after the event, memory may have distorted original feelings. But since he was only twelve at the time, it seems safe to say that whatever Gottlober actually felt was strongly influenced by parental and social expectations. In the eighteenth century, Solomon Maimon, also no apologist for traditional practices, similarly relates developing an affection for a girl of his age (around eleven at the time) when a marriage between them seemed in the offing.[11] Finally, Jacob Emden, one of the chief spokesmen for orthodoxy in eighteenth century Germany, seems to have fallen in love with the daughter of a wealthy Emden Jew at the age of about fifteen, although his father refused to allow the match.[12] In all of these cases, private experience seems to have been molded by social expectations: young boys expected to fall in love (whatever that might have meant) in the context of the system of arranged marriages.

The Yiddish chapbook literature of Eastern Europe confirms this assumed connection between love and marriage.[13] A

remarkable tale, which is probably from the early nineteenth
century at the latest, tells of a daughter of a rabbi from
Constantinople who is betrothed to a rabbi's son from
Brisk.[14] Foreshadowing I. B. Singer's story of Yentl the
yeshivah student, the girl disguises herself as a boy and goes
to study in the yeshivah of her fiancé where she naturally falls
in love with him. Another theme which is common in this
literature is that of the boy and girl who fall in love only to
discover at the end of the story that they were destined for
each other by a vow (tekiyas kaf) between their parents. The
theme of predestination was, of course, common to early modern
European literature but it was easily assimilated into a Jewish
context. According to a number of well-known midrashim, God is
said to have engaged in matchmaking since He finished creating
the world.[15] Predestined matches gave divine legitimacy to
parental arrangements which might otherwise have seemed crudely
commercial and also seemed to guarantee love even though boy and
girl did not choose the marriage of their own free will. An
interesting example of this notion can be found in the memoir of
the eighteenth century Polish Jew, Ber of Bolochow. Ber's first
marriage ended in divorce and he comments that his wife was
evidently not his predestined one.[16] Such a formula allowed
Ber to express what we today might describe with a more
"romantic" vocabulary.

That Jewish society encouraged romantic affection prior to
marriage is supported by the common practice of allowing the
engaged couple to spend time together before the wedding. While
some of these meetings may have been thoroughly Platonic, there
is good evidence to suggest similarities to the "bundling"
practices common in early modern France and North America.[17]
Bundling was a part of courtship in which some sexual contact
short of intercourse took place between the couple. The
seventeenth century moralist Isaiah Horowitz denounced the
custom but revealed that other authorities may well have
countenanced it:

> Avoid very carefully allowing the bride and groom to sit
> together before the wedding as is the custom in this wicked
> generation. For not only do they sit together, but he even
> hugs and kisses her . . . and I am appalled at the
> authorities of this generation who tolerate this great
> iniquity . . . For, even if she is still a minor, the
> groom's lust will overcome him as a result of his love and
> he might have an ejaculation . . . and even if he does not
> ejaculate, in any case, it would be impossible for him to
> avoid having an erection.[18]

Horowitz is primarily concerned with the sexual transgressions which might result from the "hugging and kissing" before the wedding (he probably means during the period of engagement rather than immediately before the wedding). He appears to distinguish between the sexual lust that could lead to these transgressions and the love which he assumes develops between the engaged couple. Love may lead to lust and therefore the couple should not be allowed such physical intimacy. But Horowitz doesn't not seem to denounce the love itself: he assumes it en passant as a natural (if, perhaps, not universal) product of engagement.

Horowitz was from Prague and he may well be reporting practices common in that area and probably also in areas to the east. In the eighteenth century, Ezekiel Landau, also of Prague, reports a case in which this "Jewish bundling" practice led to full-fledged intercourse: "[He] was accustomed to spending time with her [his fiancée] since he traveled from place to place on business and would stop in the apartment of the bride's father for several days in the middle of his journeys . . . [S]he had intercourse with him several times and became pregnant by him. [The groom told the rabbi] that the bride had had no intimate contact with any other man, but only with him [as a result] of the love which was between them . . ."[19] The circumstances of the case suggest a reasonably well-off family, thus refuting the presumption that such practices were limited to the less educated, poorer classes. Unless the parents exercised little control in their household, they would certainly have known that the engaged couple was together. From this and a good many other cases of premarital sex between engaged couples, it appears that such intimacy was not entirely deviant. For our purposes, what is important is the admission in this case by the groom that his relations with his fiancée were a result of the love which had developed between them before the marriage.

It would be difficult to develop a history of this bundling practice. In the sixteenth century, Moses Isserles (d. 1572) discusses a case from Cracow in which a girl comes to live either with or in the house of her fiancé.[20] The legal question is unrelated to this arrangement and Isserles makes no comment about the relations between the couple. This is an argument from silence and we cannot know for sure what Isserles thought about such premarital contact. We do have evidence from the nineteenth century memoirs, which were typically written by those who came from rabbinic or householder families, that grooms and brides met only on the day of their wedding. Perhaps Horowitz's critique of "Jewish bundling" and similar rabbinic strictures had an effect on at least the upper classes. But if such behavior persisted among members of other classes, we may have an example of how deviant behavior can reveal a wider range of possibilities than the practices of the literate class, that is, the class which left a direct record of its own values.

The cases of clandestine marriage which we find in the legal literature hint at the role of love in marriages, in these cases marriages against social convention. In the legislation of the communal and supra-communal councils of Poland and Lithuania, we find repeated and vociferous attempts to curb clandestine marriages.[21] A particular problem in at least the seventeenth and eighteenth centuries occurred when sons or daughters of wealthy families fell in love with servants or apprentices. In one such case from the seventeenth century, Yair Chaim Bachrach of Germany specifically allows the marriage, although he could have easily found grounds to annul it. The story is recounted with great literary flair and it could nicely find its place in the literature of romantic love. Here one has the sense that the rabbi may have sympathized with the romantic feelings of the case.[22]

If love was indeed part of the expectations inculcated in young people, it could, of course, come into conflict with parental control of marriage. The legislative attempts to control clandestine marriage reflect the desire to leave the politics of marriage in the hands of parents. Perhaps the practice most strikingly singular to the Jews to control marriage and prevent free choice was very early marriage. If love was allowed any existence in this society, it could not be connected with freedom of choice which might be a problem with children as they grew older. Although peasants in Eastern Europe tended to marry quite young, the evidence suggests that the Jewish age of marriage was considerably younger.[23] Among the elite, it was frequently thirteen or fourteen for boys and a year younger for girls.[24] But even among the lower classes, it may have also been quite young, if not as young as this. Thus, a communal regulation from Lithuania in the seventeenth century stipulates that dowry money will be provided for poor girls if they first do a stint as servants from the ages of twelve to fifteen.[25] In addition, child marriages (below thirteen for boys) were not uncommon in Eastern Europe, at least

among the rabbinic classes.[26] The social consequence of this
practice was to preclude the possibility of free choice; love
might be permitted within the context of the arranged marriage,
even in the very early ones, but not outside it.

We might very well ask how such very early marriages could
be associated with love. Certainly the enormous social
pressures attendant upon such marriages must have produced both
sexual and emotional traumas in these barely pubescent
children. Ezekiel Landau relates a particularly heartbreaking
case of a twelve-year-old boy forced to have intercourse with
his similarly young wife. Following the aborted act, the two
refused to touch each other and the boy disappeared at age
fourteen.[27] Yet, much of the evidence points to surprisingly
successful early marriages. The best known case is that of
Glückel of Hameln whose seventeenth century memoir is replete
with expressions of love toward her husband and children that
seem quite at variance to the lack of sentiment that some
historians of the family ascribe to the same period.[28] From
the end of the eighteenth century in Galicia, we hear of a minor
who sleeps with his wife on a number of occasions even though
the two continue to live with their respective parents.[29]
There is no evidence of coercion and one has the sense that the
relations between the two followed an entirely accepted
pattern. In the hagiographical collection of Hasidic stories,
Shivhei ha-Besht, the widowed son of the Maggid of Mezeritch
marries a twelve-year-old girl and is reported to have become
"very fond" of his young bride.[30] Although these stories are
legendary, they provided models for the normative values of the
Hasidim. Interestingly enough, in this tale, the mother of the
bride is initially reluctant to betroth her daughter at such a
young age, suggesting that early marriage was not automatically
accepted but was rather the consequence of social pressure. But
the lesson of the story, for our purposes, is that love was a
recognized part of marriage and even of very early marriage.

The expectation that love would develop in arranged
marriages probably acted as a self-fulfilling prophecy in at
least some cases. Just as novels of romantic love in the
eighteenth and nineteenth centuries caused people to experience
what they had read about in books, so the values of traditional
society no doubt influenced behavior and experience. Today we
tend to be shocked at the idea of marrying "mere" children and
skeptical that such marriages could work. In part, our
attitudes have been shaped by the writings of those Eastern

European maskilim, to whom we shall return, who turned their own bitter experiences of early marriage into a denunciation of the whole institution. Although some marriages failed (and we have no way of estimating what percentage), it was not necessarily because the system suppressed or denied the importance of the emotional component in marriage. While biology dictates puberty, culture shapes the emotional readiness to marry and it appears that most Jewish children, upon reaching puberty, had developed romantic desires which they expected would be fulfilled through an early marriage.

The material that I have presented here suggests that the model of "erotic modernization" proposed by historians such as Stone and Shorter does not coincide well with the experience of the Jews. Although the official value system of Ashkenazic Judaism, as expressed in legal codes, moralistic treatises and marriage manuals, seems to have placed little explicit emphasis on love prior to and in marriage, other sources, such as responsa literature and memoirs demonstrate that romantic feelings were inculcated in young people and formed part of marital expectations. To be sure, no ideology of romantic love existed in this world, for such an ideology would have necessarily challenged parental hegemony over marriage Instead, love was integrated into the notion of predestination in marriage and made a part of the arranged early marriage. It is possible that the Jews differed significantly from the societies studied by the sentiments historians, but it is more likely that the case of the Jews contributes additional questions to the validity of their conclusions. It may well be that lack of sentiment in premodern marriages is more in the eye of the historian than a reflection of historical reality.

The Haskalah and Social Reality in the Nineteenth Century

Katz was correct in arguing that the first ideology of romantic love originated with the Haskalah. The maskilim borrowed their ideas from Western literature and attacked what they took to be traditional Jewish marriage. In their desire to wrest control of marriage out of the hands of parents and traditional institutions, they contributed greatly to the image of premodern Jewish marriage as devoid of affection and based solely on economic calculations. Thus, the historians' hypothesis of loveless traditional marriages owed much to the polemics of the maskilim. Like all myths, this one had certain roots in reality, although a more limited reality than the maskilim believed.

Much of the Haskalah attack on premodern marriage seems to
have come out of generalizations from Hasidism. Indeed, to no
small extent, the Haskalah succeeded in turning Hasidism, or at
least its image of Hasidism, into the equivalent of all medieval
Judaism. In addition to its broadsides against the hypocrisy of
the Hasidic rebbes and other similar criticisms, the Haskalah
attacked the Hasidim for marrying their children very early.
Although the ideal and practice of early marriage seem to have
been widespread among all segments of the Eastern European
Jewish community and to have predated Hasidism by many
centuries, the evidence indicates that the Hasidim probably
continued the custom longer than other Jews. Thus, most of the
cases of child marriage (i.e. under thirteen for boys) which I
have uncovered from the nineteenth century and which may serve
as an index for early marriage in general, appear in the
responsa of Hasidic rabbis.[31]

Hasidism may also have provided the maskilim with the model
for a sexually repressive Judaism. Hasidism did not break with
the normative Jewish insistence on marriage, but it seems to
have urged a much more ascetic attitude in marriage than was
earlier the norm. In the Shivhei ha-Besht, one finds a number
of different stories of saints who abstain from sex with their
wives for long periods, a practice which has virtually no
precedent in the earlier traditions.[32] In extreme statements
such as one finds in Elimelech of Lizensk and Nachman of
Bratslav there is a sense of negation not only of erotic
feelings but of any marital affection at all.[33] No doubt such
positions must have found little resonance among the average
Hasidim, but they do suggest the ideal toward which at least the
zaddikim strove. Since there are also indications of affection
in marriage in the Baal Shem Tov stories, we must be cautious in
generalizing about Hasidism, but as a preliminary hypothesis, it
seems plausible that at least some tendencies in Hasidism were
much more repressive than Ashkenazic Judaism in general.

A possible confirmation of this suggestion can be found in
the anti-Hasidic polemics of Joseph Perl. In his Megalleh
Temirin, Perl accused the Hasidim of licentiousness and
promiscuity. He also attacked Hasidic theology, which was based
on the Kabbalah, as pornographic.[34] Yet, these claims, which
find no support in the actual history of Hasidism, may actually
prove the opposite: since Perl's intent was to demonstrate the
hypocrisy of the Hasidim, it made sense for him to accuse them
of doing the opposite of their official ideology. For Perl, the

repressive nature of Hasidism was so obvious that the best way to satirize it was to portray the Hasidim as promiscuous. Elsewhere, Perl claims that Hasidism broke up the traditional Jewish family since the Hasidim were always off at the courts of the zaddikim, leaving wives and children behind.[35] This argument may have some truth in it and it would be worthwhile to investigate the impact of Hasidism on the Jewish family. If Perl was right about Hasidism's subversion of the family then it may be possible to conclude that the male fellowship provided by the Hasidic court provided an escape from family life.

Whether or not Hasidism was in reality as hostile to love in marriage as the maskilim believed, it provided the Haskalah with useful ammunition. But the romantic ideology of the maskilim was even more the product of the biographies of the maskilim themselves. The memoir literature of the nineteenth century Haskalah revolves around the unhappy early marriages of the heroes who frequently either divorce or leave their wives when they discover the Haskalah. As I have argued elsewhere,[36] there is a strong connection in these works between unsuccessful marriages and adoption of Haskalah ideology. It is just possible that one factor that predisposed young intellectuals to drift toward Western ideas of Enlightenment was unhappiness with their adolescence, spent with a strange young wife in the often tyrannical household of their in-laws. Enlightenment, including the ideal of romantic love, formed an attractive escape from this oppressive reality.

No ideological avenues of escape existed for earlier youths whose marriages had failed. Like the fourteen-year old we encountered in the eighteenth century who disappeared from the house of his in-laws, flight or perhaps divorce were purely personal solutions. Hasidism may have fulfilled a similar role for young men caught in unhappy marriages, although this was but one factor among many in the rise of the movement. The Haskalah offered an ideology with which to counter traditional marriage. This ideology sought to redefine adolescence as a period when marriage could not succeed and when time should be devoted to other pursuits such as education or acquisition of a career. In this, the maskilim only borrowed from the new definiton of adolescence which began to emerge in Europe in the eighteenth and nineteenth centuries,[37] but they applied it to the Jewish situation.

The memoirs of the maskilim suggest that most early marriages were unhappy. This testimony is suspect in the light of the evidence we have already examined from early modern times. We have seen that the traditional understanding of adolescence prepared many, although certainly not all, boys and girls for marriage and sexuality at the time of puberty. Like all ideologies, the Haskalah tended to generalize the conditions out of which it emerged and the maskilim created a myth of the unhappy early marriage based on their own experience. Undoubtedly, those who accepted the new values of romantic love and a free adolescence were much more likely to experience their own early marriages as oppressive: in this way, an ideology can become a self-fulfilling prophecy. But it would be a mistake to read back into history the perceptions of the nineteenth century maskilim.

The tragic youths of the maskilim, whether products of ideology or reality, foreclosed the possibility of love. Although captivated by Western Romantic literature, the young Jewish intellectuals were rarely able to realize the ideals they read about in their own lives. They suffered from a high divorce rate and many would no doubt have agreed with Abraham Mapu that "only one in a thousand will derive joy from family life and even that will be a facade."[38]

In this respect, art followed life. Up through the 1860s or so, Haskalah literature in both Hebrew and Yiddish was heavily didactic. The maskilim advocated a new capitalist mentality to replace the medieval commercial ethic of the Jews. In fiction such as Israel Aksenfeld's Dos Shterntikhl (1840s) and Mendele's Ha-Avot ve-ha-Banim (1868), the old system of marriage symbolizes medieval commercial values.[39] Capitalism required the "decommercialization" of marriage, which meant that instead of a business deal between parents, marriage would be contracted freely between the young people themselves. These authors wedded romantic love to capitalism in order to remove marriage from the marketplace. However, in such didactic novels, romance is really not the main theme, but rather exists as an artificial prop for the main Haskalah ideology of economic productivity. Novels treating love more centrally, such as Mapu's Ahavat Zion, are typically set in an imaginary biblical past and thus have a quality of escapism about them.

By the 1870s and 1880s, Hebrew and Yiddish literature had become less didactic and more realistic. But love remained elusive and, as Baruch Kurzweil shrewdly observed, the heroes of many of these stories seem caught in perpetual adolescence, unable to realize mature erotic relationships.[40] Sholem

Aleichem spoke for a whole generation when he said that the peculiar problem of the Jewish writer was to "write a novel without romance."[41] For these intellectuals, the social reality of the Jews did not include love.

Yet, it is crucial for the historian not to be misled by either the fiction or the ideology of the nineteenth century intellectuals. Their personal reality was not the reality of all the Jews. We may, in fact, be able to learn much more about the values of late nineteenth century Jews not by reading the literary giants but by examining the voluminous writings of pulp novelists like A. M. Dik and Shomer.[42] These best-selling authors, who were denouced for writing trash by the "better" writers such as Sholem Aleichem, undoubtedly had more influence on popular culture than did their critics. Dik and Shomer fed their readers an unending stream of the Jewish equivalent of Harlequin romances. As David Roskies has shown, many of Dik's stories differed little from the earlier Yiddish chapbook literature, but where the earlier stories were usually built around predestined matches, Dik infiltrated Haskalah values by putting the young couple more fully in control of their fate.[43] It was in this literature that Jews could find modern values of romantic love, but the form of the literature was so close to more traditional models that it represents less of a revolution than an evolution in values.

Even before industrialization and emigration began to have a major effect on the Jewish family at the end of the nineteenth century, a quiet transformation was taking place within the traditional world. Probably independent of Haskalah polemics, orthodox Jews were beginning to change their attitudes toward age of marriage. Moses Feivish (1817-1887), the author of a popular treatise on the laws of marriage, condemned marriage of boys at age thirteen. He held that sexual development was not as precocious in his time as it was earlier so that early marriage was not necessary to protect against sin. Feivish recommended marriage at age eighteen, since "the main part of one's studying should be during these years. [Therefore, the rabbis] allowed one to wait until this age."[44] Feivish's prescriptions are particularly striking because they may have been related to his own biography. He was married at age fourteen and ran off to a Vilna yeshivah with his young wife because his in-laws refused to let him study.[45]

Feivish represents the shift towards study as the correct activity during adolescence. A similar position was taken by

Naphtali Zvi Berlin, the head of the great Volozhin yeshiva for much of the nineteenth century. In his commentary on Exodus 1:7, Berlin wrote: ". . . girls who begin to give birth when they are young (be'neur'ei'hen) become weak and sickly. And the same is true of males who use their sexual organs for procreation in the days of their youth. They become weak in health . . ."[46] The health argument for later marriage can already be found in eighteenth century writings, such as Jacob Emden's response, but Berlin's position took on institutional meaning. The Lithuanian yeshivot did not accept married men with their wives and it was only in 1879 that the kolel was established as an institution for married students. A special category of students were perushim, those who had separated from their wives in order to study. As Shaul Stampfer has shown, the age of marriage among the yeshivah students rose dramatically in the second half of the nineteenth century until it stood at around twenty-five.[47] Thus, by putting study before marriage, the yeshivah movement, which was a nineteenth century phenomenon, may have contributed to the rise in age of marriage. With the claim that young boys were not sexually ready for marriage, the very definition of adolescence changed and, with it, the expectations placed on children reaching puberty.

One of the major summaries of Jewish law from the end of the nineteenth century and beginning of the twentieth confirms this shift in priorities. In 1905, Yehiel Michael Epstein (1829-1908) published his Arukh Ha-Shulhan on the Even Ha-Ezer (laws of marriage) section of the Shulhan Arukh. He states explicitly that one should wed at eighteen and study before. Echoing the argument we found in Feivish, he claims that "the instincts have weakened in these generations" so that marriage to avoid masturbation and temptation is less necessary. Epstein thoroughly rejects the earlier Ashkenazic tradition which allowed child marriage and concludes: "And there is not reason to discuss this matter at length since it is virtually non-existent in our time."[48]

Within the orthodox world, then, changes in values similar to those advocated by the Haskalah were taking place which may have affected secular demographic trends. An older average age of marriage did not in and of itself herald a breakdown in parental authority, but it did create a period after puberty, which we today call adolescence, that was not constrained by marriage. Since parental control was exercised by supervising the match of children and then boarding them in one of the parental houses for a set period, delay in marriage would create the possibility of children leaving home following puberty, especially if they went off to study.

As the age of marriage rose, children of orthodox families were able to exercise greater choice in mates, even if parents continued to arrange the match. Thus, Solomon Schwadron (d. 1911) reported the following case from Galicia:

> . . . the groom objects in front of a number of people and he also says to his mother that he has not yet seen the face of the bride. [But] since it is the father's custom to intimidate the household, they were afraid to tell him [of the son's objections] and they wrote the contract of engagement. And, now, the groom has seen the bride and he does not like her since she is very short and not pretty and is a bit repulsive . . .[49]

In addition to a fleeting portrait of a strict patriarchal household, we learn from this responsum that a meeting between bride and groom before the engagement would not have been out of the question if the father were not so forbidding. It is also interesting to observe from Schwadron's ruling, in which he allows the engagement to be broken without penalty, that the wishes of the son should have been taken into account. Schwadron sympathizes with the boy's rejection of the girl based on her appearance and quotes from the Song of Songs to the effect that height is one of the traits desirable in the bride.

In other cases, children tried to arrange their own marriages. Here is a case from 1879 reported by Abraham Landau Bornstein of Sochaczew (1839-1910):

> The boy Chaim said that for a long time, perhaps four or five years, the soul of the virgin (Nehama) had adhered to him in love . . . and once the two of them were by coincidence in the community of Likewe (?) and they talked together day and night. She said to him that it seemed to her that their love was eternal. During this whole time, she wrote him many letters containing statements of love and affection (ahavah ve'hibba) and in one of the letters she wrote that he should find a way of avoiding an engagement with another since she would certainly find some trick to become his wife, even though she was already engaged to someone else.[50]

There was nothing new about such clandestine love, but there are some peculiarly modern elements to this case. The boy and girl meet in a community to which each has traveled, which suggests greater mobility than would have been the case for early adolescents. Like Mendelssohn's letters to his fiancée, these letters are not copies from letter formularies but are spontaneous expressions of affection, something that would have been extremely unusual in an earlier period when most letter writing of this sort followed strict conventions. The use of words like ahavah also suggests modern influence, perhaps from the Yiddish pulp literature.

Similarly, Pauline Wengeroff, the daughter of a wealthy Lithuanian family, exchanged intimate letters with her fiancé in 1849.[51] Wengeroff's engagement was arranged by the parents, but it had certain clearly modern elements such as the exchange of real rather than formulaic letters. In addition, Wengeroff was allowed to meet privately with her husband-to-be, which, as we have seen, was part of traditional engagement customs in an earlier time. But in Wengeroff's circles, the practice had thoroughly disappeared, even if it possibly persisted among less educated and less wealthy people. Wengeroff attributes the increased freedom to the influence of non-Jewish ideas and she points out that her sister, married just a few years earlier, only met her husband the day of the wedding. Here is a case of the reintroduction of traditional practices, which had been suppressed, as a result of Western notions of romantic love.

These cases, taken from orthodox settings, suggest the complicated way in which old customs were giving way to new. Even among those who had seemingly moved away from traditional attitudes, many of the old practices persisted. Thus, Y.L. Peretz's father, who was a maskil, arranged his son's marriage in the traditional fashion.[52] In a letter formulary from the beginning of the twentieth century, a young man writes to a matchmaker for help in securing the parent's approval for his prospective marriage.[53] Here the young people have taken the initiative by falling in love in the "modern style" but they turn to a traditional institution to put the marriage on the right basis.

Was there, then, a Jewish revolution of romantic sentiment? The answer is ambiguous at best. Love was not absent from marriage in early modern Jewish society, despite the effects of early marriage. Nor was love necessarily a deviation from a system of instrumental marital norms: it was, rather, an expected part of this system. Parents generally controlled marriage but their control was by no means absolute and the degree of freedom within the system allowed for the possibility of love, whether sanctioned or illicit.

The Eastern European enlighteners tried to introduce Western values of romantic love and free choice in marriage, but, on a personal level, their attempted revolution must be judged a failure. Their inability to realize love in their own lives led to a bitter critique of traditional Jewish society and the creation of an extreme image of the nature of Jewish marriage. It was on the more popular level, in pulp literature that wedded Western ideas with indigenous Jewish traditions, that new values began to take root. Yet, more than a revolution in values, the modernization of Jewish marriage was a result of the victory of love once parental control of marriage dissipated. If love had always played a role in marriage, it could only become the main element when urbanization and emigration at the end of the nineteenth century weakened the power of the traditional family. As Jews increasingly left their families before marriage, whether to study or work, they removed love from its traditional matrix and made it the centerpiece of their emotional lives, thus replacing the "family of origin" with the "family of procreation."[54] Only once this shift in power from one generation to the next had been completed could love acquire a new and autonomous meaning.

SECULAR RELIGIOSITY: REFLECTIONS ON POST-TRADITIONAL JEWISH SPIRITUALITY AND COMMUNITY

Paul R. Mendes-Flohr
Hebrew University

I

The Venerable Cardinal Newman once observed that the crisis of religion in the modern world is one of "authority and obedience." The authority of religion has been eclipsed and, consequently, also obedience to its precepts and teachings. The process leading to this crisis is generally understood as that of secularization, the radical political, social and cultural change which beginning with the eighteenth century is one of the salient features of modernity, at least in the West.[1] It is as a cultural, more specifically as a cognitive process that secularization most profoundly affects and troubles religion. Philology offers us a ready insight into the nature of the process. In Medieval Latin the term saecularisatio was preeminently a juristic concept denoting the transference of Church proprety to the laity. Our contemporary use of the term, which apparently only evolved as a category of analysis in the late nineteenth century, may thus be viewed as a metaphorical extrapolation from the Medieval Latin: crucial areas of political, social and cultural life have been transferred from the domain of the "sacred" to that of the "profane." With respect to cognitive culture, authority to discern truth--moral, epistemological and ontological--has been transferred from the Church to the laity. Immanuel Kant placed the process under the rubric of autonomy: the ability and duty of the individual to use his own reason and experience to determine the nomos or laws governing truth, theoretical and practical.

The autonomous individual, as Kant himself tirelessly argued, is not necessarily ungodly or disrespectful of religious traditions. Indeed, the autonomous individual may have profoundly religious sentiments and concerns, but, and here is the rub, because of his autonomy or "secularity" the authority of the Church--and the tradition embodied by the Church--is for him no longer intellectually tenable.[2] To characterize this tension between an abiding religious sensibility and a rejection or at least questioning of the Church and tradition as the

-19-

mediators of truth, I should like to introduce the admittedly
infelicitious but I trust elucidating terms, "secular
religiosity."[3]

A secular religiosity is implicit in much of our literary
and philosophical discourse since the West embarked on the
ambiguous adventure of modernity. A secular religiosity
certainly seems to inform the dialectical reflection of Hegel,
the antinomian rantings of Nietzche, the spiritual
peregrinations of Hesse, the Angst of Heidegger, the tormented
world of Franz Kafka and the iconoclastic mysticism of A.D.
Gordon. Modern theological discourse is also often prompted by
agnostic musings of secular religiosity. For much of nineteenth
and twentieth century theology, tradition--even Scripture--is no
longer the source of ultimate authority guiding the religious
quest. Indicatively, historical revelation is all but removed
from the theologian's purview. Following Friedrich
Schleiermacher, the emphasis is on the individual's religious
experience and consciousness.[4] The ambivalence to tradition
is even more dramatically reflected in the so-called historical
theology which by employing critical scholarship or Hegelian
historiosophy sought to free religion from the encumberances of
the past by illuminating the evolutionary character of religious
consciousness.[5] To be sure, these theologians often do relate
to their respective traditions, but generally in a highly
idiosyncratic fashion, and again, these traditions do not
provide the fundamental ground for their theological reflections
and religious quest.

For any historic religious community, however, a theology
unmediated by tradition is most problematic. Indeed, it is
questionable whether a theology sans tradition can serve an
historic community. For in purely sociological terms, tradition
is the symbolic and cognitive ground of an historic community:
it is the matrix of the community's shared memory, language and
meaning structures. Hence, a "post-traditional" theology,
grounded in a secular religiosity, entails the prospect of a
cognitive disjunction--and the possible loss of a meaningful
discourse--between the theologian and his historic community.

II

Yet, a post-traditional theology presumably articulates the
spiritual situation and predicament of other members of the
theologian's historic community. It therefore may be asked

whether the theologian could serve as a spiritual leader to those members of his historic community who like himself have gone through the "purgatory" of secularization and reject or at least doubt the authority of their tradition. Can he establish with these, his secularized, post-traditional coreligionists, a theological discourse which while remaining alert to the promptings of a secular religiosity nonetheless preserves the historic community as a context for meaningful religious reflection and quest? The dilemma of a secular individual with an abiding religious sensibility--and implicitly that of the theologian faced with the challenge to relate secular religiosity to a specific religious tradition--is incisively summarized by the anthropologist Clifford Geertz:[6]

> Established connections between particular varieties of faith and the cluster of images and institutions which have classically nourished them are for certain people in certain circumstances coming unstuck. . . . The intriguing question for the anthropologist is, "How do men of religious sensibility react when the machinery of faith begins to wear out? What do they do when traditions falter?" . . . They do, of course, all sorts of things. They lose their sensibility. Or they channel it into ideological fervor. Or they adopt an imported creed. Or they turn worriedly in upon themselves, or they cling even more intensely to the faltering traditions. Or they try to rework these traditions into more effective forms. Or they split themselves in half, living spiritually in the past and physically in the present. Or they try to express their religiousness in secular activites. And a few simply fail to notice their world is moving or, noticing, just collapse . . . Given the increasing diversification of individual experience, the dazzling multiformity of which is the hallmark of modern consciousness, the task of . . . any religious tradition to inform faith of particular men and to be informed by it is becoming ever more difficult. A religion which would be catholic these days has an extraordinary variety of mentalities to be catholic about; and the question, can it do this and still remain a specific and persuasive force with a shape and identity of its own, has a steadily more problematic ring.

Secular religiosity then inheres the prospect of a spiritual solopsism:[7] bereft of tradition, religious sensibility shares the individuation and privacy of the modern world; faith is increasingly isolated from the matrix of community and the cognitive universe which Peter Berger calls a "plausibility structure" of established forms of meaning and symbolizations of reality and experience. The theologian who seeks to address the needs of a specific historic community is obviously charged with the awesome task of reversing this seemingly inexorable process.

The continuity with the community's religious heritage implied by this type of discourse obviously requires more than the commonplace cultivation of that heritage as merely a sort of ethnic folklore.[8] The challenge to the theologian would then seem to be to capture anew the cognitive and spiritual significance of his community's religious tradition, and to indicate how this tradition, unfettered by heteronomous authority, could allow the individual jealous of his intellectual and spiritual autonomy to give expression and even depth to his religious sensibilities.

The role of the theologian as a spiritual guide in this specific sense may be elucidated by the Jewish experience.[9] In classical Judaism, the preeminent type of religious teacher was the talmid chacham, the student of the Torah and Israel's revered sages.[10] It was his "great task to pass on [the Torah] and develop its meaning for his generation."[11] As a spiritual guide, the authority of the talmid chacham was hence not charismatic but hermeneutic. "He expounds the Word of God, but does not embody it."[12] The Word of God is preeminent. Even God, the rabbis tell us, studies Torah.

The modern spiritual leader--if we may state our thesis somewhat apodictically--must also be a talmid chacham, a student of the Torah and the sacred tradition of Israel. But there is an important difference between the spiritual leader of classical Judaism and that required by post-traditional Judaism. In his study of Torah, the talmid chacham of classical Judaism follows an apostolic hermeneutic: being grounded in an unambiguous conviction that Torah is the Word of God, his study and interpretative endeavor ultimately serve to proclaim the Word. In contrast, the post-traditional spiritual leader, given the epistemological agnosticism attendant to his secular religiosity, must perforce pursue a dialogical hermeneutic: he studies the Torah (qua Scripture and sacred traditions) with an existential commitment to listen attentively, prepared to respond to it as possibly the direct, living address of God. This approach, of course, was first articulated by Martin Buber and Franz Rosenzweig. These two renown twentieth century German Jewish philosophers, both of whom affirmed Judaism from the midst of secular European culture, agree in their fundamental dialogical approach to the study of Torah. Yet, as we shall see, they differed critically in their conception of Judaism, especially of Jewish tradition. Hence, they may be viewed as two alternative models for post-traditional Jews.

III

Buber would undoubtedly endorse Rosenzweig's statement that "faith based on authority is equal to unbelief" (der Autoritätsgläubige ist gleich dem Ungläubigen).[13] Faith meant for both of them a relationship to God--a relationship which had been facilitated for Jews of the past by their sacred traditions. If these traditions are to be once again meaningful for the modern Jew then the relationship which these traditions nurtured and guarded must, Buber and Rosenzweig concurred, somehow be reestablished. Although this relationship is mutual, it is, they stressed, initiated by God: God who is utterly beyond the world enters a providential relationship with it. This founding belief and experience of theistic faith, according to Rosenzweig, explains the centrality of miracles in the respective religious traditions of the West.[14] Phenomenologically understood, miracles are a prophetic sign of God's involvement in the world. Hence, as Goethe's Faust observed, "miracle is the favorite child of faith."[15] But we moderns have lost our belief in miracles and the consequence of such, Rosenzweig lamented, is a loss of our faith in God's relationship to the world. Even theologians he noted, are embarrassed by the notion of miracles. No wonder the concepts of Creation, Revelation and Redemption--if they are taken seriously and not simply as edifying metaphors--have become most uncongenial to many modern theologians. Each of these concepts seeks to clarify various aspects of God's miraculous involvement in the world. The exigent task of theology, as Rosenzweig pursued it in his Star of Redemption (1921), is to affirm the phenomenological and theological content of these concepts. This is the point of departure for Rosenzweig's encounter with theistic faith. His rejection of philosophical relativism and agnosticism was prompted by a decision to adopt what he called Offenbarungsglaube;[16] faith besed on revelation, viz., that revelation is the historic moment in the founding of theistic religion. Accordingly, he defined tradition as the living, continuously renewed witness to concrete, historic miracle.[17] Tradition is thus the context of faith. "The belief in miracle," he writes in the Star of Redemption, "and not just the belief in decorative miracles, but that in the central miracle of revelation, is to this extent a completely historical belief. Even the Lutheran reformation altered nothing in this respect. It only moved the path of personal confirmation from

the periphery of the tradition, where the present is located,
directly into the center, where the tradition originated.
Thereby it created a new believer, not a new belief. Belief
remained historically anchored. . ."[18]

Buber shared Rosenzweig's Offenbarungsglaube and belief that
tradition is the historical witness of God's relationship to the
world. They differed, however, fundamentally with respect to
which facets of the Jewish tradition can still serve to quicken
one's relationship to God. This difference was most clearly
evidenced in their famous exchange on Jewish Law.[19] Buber, as
is known, assumed a metanomian position, declaiming Jewish Law,
the mitzvoth, as a heteronomous imposition that shackles the
Jew's spontaneous relationship to God. Rosenzweig concurred
that the Law conceived simply as a legal construct is a
heteronomous distortion of religious faith, but--Rosenzweig
queried Buber--is this the Law actually lived by the Jew,
caressed and sanctified by him for millenia? Existentially, in
the lived moment of its fulfillment, Rosenzweig affirmed, the
Law may be for the Jew of faith not Gesetz, a heteronomous
legalism, but Gebot, a divine commandment which in directly
addressing the individual evokes his spontaneous response. Qua
commandment, the Law quickens the Jew's relationship to God.
Buber's "reply" to Rosenzweig was terse: The God of Revelation
is not a Gesetzgeber. He is not a Law-giver![20]

In many respects the exchange between Buber and Rosenzweig
on the Law was typical of the German-Jewish heirs of Kant's
moral philosphy.[21] At root the difference between them,
however, is their contrasting conceptions of Jewish tradition.
Early in his career Buber defined his task as identifying a
"subterranean" Jewish tradition which modern Jews estranged from
the "official" rabbinic Judaism could respond to with filial
affection and devotion.[22] It would be quick, however, to
judge Buber's conception of Judaism as wantonly arbitrary and
tendentious. As a student of Wilhelm Dilthey he read texts as a
Lebensphilosoph, endeavoring to distill through a personal,
empathic Nacherleben (re-experiencing) the life-moments that
gave birth to the text. Using this method Buber sought to
identify the kerygmatic core of Judaism which he understood to
be the ontological possibility, first proclaimed in the Hebrew
Scripture, of a dialogical encounter between man and God. In
Buber's judgment, only certain texts within the literary corpus
of Judaism bear witness to the founding and authenticating
kerygma of Judaism. Due to its obsessive legalism, rabbinic

Judaism, which set the normative contours of Jewish tradition, Buber held, obscured the primal Jewish alertness to the Biblical kerygma. Judaism's primal spiritual sensibility, however, remained alive, leading as it were an underground existence, manifesting itself in select individuals and in movements such as early Beshtian Hasidism. Without attempting to evaluate Buber's method or the validity of his understanding of Jewish spirituality, in particular rabbinic, we may note that by his own admission his presentation of Judaism is highly selective; only certain aspects, and at times surprising aspects of Judaism, qualify as exemplifications of authentic Judaism. Hence, it may be asked whether Buber's conception of a counter-Jewish tradition, irrespective of its theological merits, has the inherent capacity to speak to all but a select number of Jews. For the community of Jews at large, even if they are ambivalent heirs to the rabbinic tradition, it is this tradition which provides their identity and self-recognition as a community.[23] In other words, the sacrality of a tradition, as Durkheim noted, has a sociological dimension. Hence, inasmuch as a critically edited text is not the text of any historic community, except perhaps that of scholars,[24] so Buber's "counter-tradition" is not, indeed cannot be the tradition of the historic Jewish community. Bereft of sociological sacrality, Buber's Judaism could only speak to select Jews, or perhaps rather to select aspects within the soul and spiritual imagination of many modern Jews. It could not, however, provide the basis of a communal identity. This is indeed ironic for one such as Buber who was so passionately devoted to the renewal of Jewish community.

Rosenzweig's attitude to and ergo conception of Jewish tradition is radically different from Buber's. His view of Judaism is summarized in his statement, "nothing Jewish is alien to me."[25] He included within the purview of this statement, Jewish cuisine, gestures and, of course, more significantly the oral, extra-scriptual traditions which filled and permeated the whole consciousness of the traditional Jewish community. The oral traditions, which animate the life and soul of the Jewish community, are in Rosenzweig's view prior to and more fundamental than Scripture and other sacred texts. To be sure, the oral traditions attest the sacred texts of Judaism. But it is more comprehensive than these texts, for the oral traditions embrace a mass of ritual and religious usage, of customs and rules, which are at best adumbrated in the sacred texts. The oral traditions articulate the sacred texts, rendering the written Word spoken and alive in the life of the Jew. Hence, the sacred texts of Judaism, according to Rosenzweig, must be read or rather lived from within the oral traditions of the Jewish community. To abstract them from this context is to deny them of their extensive religious significance. The first steps in this existential journey into traditional Judaism (which followed his theological clarification and affirmation of the concepts of Creation, Revelation, and Redemption, that is, after having completed the Star of Redemption) were to set-up a Jewish household--to keep a kosher kitchen and other sancta of traditional Jewish family life--but also to appropriate the religious gestures of everyday Jewish life, prayer and the fulfillment of the mitzvoth. His initial focus was the traditional liturgy, wherein he discovered, as he states already in the Star of Redemption, the fulcrum of Jewish spirituality. Not surprisingly, the extra-liturgical mitzvoth were more difficult for him to comprehend and adopt, but gradually he did so.[26] To be sure, his relationship to liturgy and the mitzvoth remained dialogical; but it was a dialogue from within traditional Jewish praxis. Rosenzweig lived as a traditional Jew in order to appropriate the spiritual reality of the tradition, to know it, as he once put it, hymnically.[27]

The unheralded response of German Jewry (and today American and French Jewry) to Rosenzweig is an ample testimony of his role as a spiritual guide. The response to him has little to do with his Star of Redemption--few read it and fewer understand it; nor can the response be explained by the charismatic, saintly quality of his life. Rather, we surmise, it is the nature of his return, from the midst of secular European culture, to traditional Judaism which is paradigmatic to a post-traditional Jewry seeking renewed Jewish community and spirituality. Rosenzweig, however, disappoints these Jews in one very serious way. He suggests that Jewish spirituality demands that the Jews withdraw from history and that they become meta-historic guardians of the promise of an absolute future, of a future beyond the wiles of history. It has thus been rightly observed that Rosenzweig is the last great Jewish philosopher of the Diaspora--but not simply in the sense that he did not witness the Jews' return (as sovereign actors) into history through the establishment of the State of Israel. Prompted by his eagerness to accept the inner reality of the traditional Jewish community, Rosenzweig also affirmed its detachment, as it

evolved in the Diaspora, from history. This indifference to
history and the fate of the rest of humanity was a posture
typical of the pre-modern world; it reflected the political and
social reality of a stratified, insulated Medieval world. With
the rise of the modern order this reality began to change
rapidly. As Rosenzweig himself recognizes in his early
writings, the modern world gave birth to a new sense of Ökumene,
of a shared universe and the attendant demand for a responsible
and active involvement in the shaping of the evolving
Ökumene.[28] Alongside this changed perception of history and
politics, traditional Judaism seemed locked to a more parochial
view of history. Thus as many Jews entered the modern world and
adopted its political ethos, often with a unique passion,
traditional Judaism seemed ever so anachronistic. Rosenzweig,
of course, was aware of this perplexity regarding the abiding
particularity of traditional Judaism, Indeed he shared it; he
overcame it by celebrating the a-historical posture of "the
Synagogue" as a metaphysical virute: content with its unique
relationship with the God of Eternity and standing beyond
history--viz., politics and war--the Synagogue exemplifies the
Messianic promise and thereby prods the Church, enmeshed in
history, to lead history beyond itself to the eschaton.
Meanwhile, the Synagogue is to look inward in blissful seclusion
from the world.[29] There is a compelling sublimity to this
perception of Israel's destiny, but it is also profoundly
distressing. For it suggests that isolation from the world is
an intrinsic quality of traditional Jewish spiritualy.
Notwithstanding his ascription of a dialectical, eschatological
significance to the Synagogue's seclusion, Rosenzweig's
celebration of an indifference to history is offensive to the
modern Jew immersed in the urgencies of both Jewish and world
history.

Buber was more alert to this aspect of the modern Jewish
sensibility. As a Zionist, he appreciated the need to relieve
the social and political distress of the Jews. He also
understood the call of the "secular city" and accordingly sought
to free religious faith from its fear of the profane and to
render it relevant to the political and social challenges of the
modern world. Thus his pan-sacramentalism and religious
socialism with their demand that faith be extended beyond the
confines of the ecclesia to our public and political
activity--provinces of life hitherto all too often abandoned to
instrumental aims and cynicism. The true challenge of religious

faith is to affirm God in the "broken" world of the everyday. "We can only work for the Kingdom of God," Buber writes, "through working in all spheres allotted to us. . . . One cannot say we must work here and not there, this leads to the goal and that does not. . . . There is no legitimately messianic politics, but that does not exclude politics from the sphere of the hallowing."[30] Buber unceasingly argued that this approach to the "secular city" and politics was consistent with the traditional Jewish refusal to acknowledge any intrinsically profane sphere and the concomitant commandment to sanctify all of life.

Buber's religious socialism acquired a specifically Jewish expression in his Zionism. The return to Zion, he taught, will restore to Israel the conditions enabling her to realize, under the conditions of autonomous Jewish existence, her vocation to exemplify the ideal of hallowing everyday life and the creation of a just and genuine community. "The supernational task of the Jewish people," Buber stresses, "cannot be properly accomplished unless natural life is reconquered."[31] By attending to their own historical and social needs the Jews as a community will be able to serve the rest of humanity. We do not want Palestine, Buber proclaimed, for the Jews alone, but rather for all of humanity!

Secular religiosity, as previously suggested, is a phenomenon inherent in the individuation of society and culture characteristic of modernity. As Peter Berger observes in his most recent book, The Heretical Imperative,[32] the modern world beckons us all, including the religious individual, to "heresy"--choice (the Greek verb hairein means to choose), choice before the richness of universal human experience. Open to a multiplicity of experiences and cultural options, the modern individual can no longer delimit his experience and culture to that of his primordial community. The heretical imperative, as Berger acknowledges, is thus hardly conducive to community, certainly not a community based on the considerations of historic continuity and tradition.[33] With respect to religious experience and culture, the heretical imperative sunders, liberates, Berger would say, faith from the bonds of community. In the Jewish context, the implications of this tension between faith and community are already manifest with Moses Mendelssohn (1729-1786), "the first modern Jew." In his attempt to demonstrate the compatibility of Judaism with Deism--that is, the conviction that the intellect is in the

universal, natural domain--Mendelssohn in effect rendered
Judaism a confessional religion, solely bound by a unique body
of ceremonial laws; the Jews, he insisted, have no special claim
on truth and, by implication, on the shaping of history
according to God's truth. The Jew was now free to be a
European, to accept the culture and history, that is, secular
destiny of Europe. Although he would be loath to admit it,
Mendelssohn's confessional God was no longer the God of Israel
who had entered into a covenant with the Jewish People governing
not only their mode of worship, but also their destiny--and
through them ultimately the destiny of humanity--in history.
The Covenant, as the authenticating ground of Jewish community,
entails more than confessional ritual and belief, but a
sustained responsibility to creation and history.[34] However,
to Mendelssohn and his heirs--as to all modern Jews to an
extent--Jewish community had become theologically problematic.

The problem implicit in the separation of Jewish faith from
the historical destiny of the Jewish people--a relationship
traditionally provided by the concept of the Covenant--may be
summarized in the question: is Jewish community, bereft of its
convenental dimension, simply the source of the Jew's mode of
worship and primary social identity? As a description of a
social fact, this is undoubtedly an adequate characterization of
the function of Jewish community. But if the issue is the
spiritual and religious significance or purpose[35] of Jewish
community, then the above characterization is not adequate. And
should it be argued, as Mendelssohn would have, that the Jewish
community is the social basis of the Jewish religion, one may
legitimately query: Why be Jewish? As citizens of the modern
world, jealous of our autonomy and intellectual integrity, the
modern Jew would have difficulty accepting the answer ultimately
implied by Mendelssohn: because God commnaded us! A Judaism
compelled by obligation, even when accompanied by an appeal to
filial and ethnic loyalty, has not worn well with the modern
sensibility.[36]

Surely the question of the modern individual's commitment to
Judaism qua a community of faith has to be pursued
existentially, that is, the individual has to discover within
Jewish religious community a spiritual meaning relevant to his
own existence. For the individual Jew who stands critically
before his ancestral tradition, the spiritual and existential
significance of Judaism must first be illuminated.
Notwithstanding their limitations, Buber and Rosenzweig serve

these individuals as spiritual guides, for both recognized that the spiritual significance of Judaism as a personal faith is grounded in the communal experience of the convenantal relationship (although each understands the Covenant and the nature of Jewish destiny rather differently). Both return to the Biblical teaching, often obscured in modern Jewish thought, that the Jewish people was born of and with the Covenant, that Judaism is not simply the religion of the Jewish people, but rather it is the religious dimension of the Jewish people.[37] The Covenant, as viewed and lived by Buber and Rosenzweig, is the supreme dialogical moment in which God addressed the House of Israel and pari passu the individual Jew. Thus, existentially, the individual Jew discovers the spiritual meaning of his own existence in the spiritual purpose and vocation of the Jewsih people. By conceiving the Covenant as primarily a dialogue, Buber and Rosenzweig helped illuminate the delicate spiritual fabric underlining the heteronomous structure of classical Judaism. They thus encouraged the renewal of a covenantal consciousness among modern Jews who otherwise feared that Jewish religious existence involved a forfeiture of their autonomy and secular dignity.

Buber and Roisenzweig profoundly appreciated the predicament of the modern Jew caught between the imperatives of secular religiosity and a primordial urging to ground his spirituality in the religious community of his forefathers. Buber and Rosenzweig knew this predicament; each sought to resolve it with integrity, with full respect for the scruples and passions of the modern sensibility and to the nuanced meaning of Judaism. Neither Buber nor Rosenzweig was dogmatic; they humbly invited us to listen in on their dialogue with God. For this invitation we are ever grateful.

JUDAISM AND MARXISM: ON THE NECESSITY OF DIALOGUE

Michael N. Dobkowski
Hobart and William Smith Colleges

Given several decades of fruitful dialogue, it should be
possible for Judaism to benefit from some of the theological and
political developments which have transpired in Christianity,
especially in terms of the bridge of dialogue and communication
being built between Christianity, Marxism and movements of
liberation. World War Two and post-war upheavals impacted
directly upon Christian theology which was radicalized through
its   exposure   to   Hitler,   Vietnam   and   the   Third   World
Revolutions. As a result of this experience, radical Christian
thinkers   entered   into   a   dialogue   with   atheistic   and
revolutionary Marxism. Both sides agreed to overlook the
profound structural differences between the two systems of
thought. Both sides, theists and materialists, agreed to
overlook the difficult problem of God's existence, and to
concentrate   instead   on   the   paramount   struggle   for   human
dignity.[1]

This dialogue has been initiated successfully because in the
contemporary world, radical Christianity and Marxism have shared
a common set of theoretical assumptions. Because radical
Christianity has de-emphasized the theistic and focused instead
on the political, both Marxists and radical Christians can talk
of the future, of a world in the state of transformation. A
doctrine of immanence has become common to both. Marxism speaks
in terms of unalienated labor. Work should be the active
relatedness of individual to nature, the creation of a new
world, including the transformation of the individual himself
through creative work. Radical Christianity speaks in terms of
ethical praxis, the belief that only human action can redeem the
world. Marxism's aim, fundamentally, is the "spiritual"
emancipation of the individual, of his liberation from the
fetters   of   economic   oppression   and   determination,   of
reconstituting the individual in his human wholeness, of
enabling him to find unity and harmony with his fellow man and
with nature. Radical Christianity's aim is the achievement of
both spiritual and temporal liberation. Both stress the role of
human activity, of man as the responsible causal agent, the
motivating   force   behind   either   the   spiritual   or   temporal
reconstruction of the world.

It is in this spirit that it may now be the appropriate moment for a Jewish-Marxist dialogue, a conversation between Jewish theism and Jewish radicalism, made even more imperative because of the Holocaust. Philosophically, an opening to the left is necessary. In spite of the fact that Marxist theorists have made significant contributions in such fields as historiography, economic and political theory, philosophy, psychology and literary criticism, a glance at even quite contemporary scholarly and influential works of biblical and talmudic criticism, Jewish history, theology and philosophy, suggests that Jewish thinkers and scholars do not regard it as incumbent upon them to take the "fact" of Marxist theory seriously into account.[2] In a word, there is a curious disparity between contemporary Jewry's practical, political obsession with Marxism in terms of global politics, world revolution, the Palestinian problem, etc., and its theoretical indifference. This neglect is doubtless partly attributable to the implacable hostility with which Marxism and Judaism have usually confronted each other, beginning with responses to Marx's essay, "On the Jewish Question." In it, Marx argued that the emancipation of the Jews depended on the emancipation of mankind from Judaism. Marx was for socialism and against capitalism. The final enemy in the final conflict was the bourgeoisie, and the Jews were the paradigm of the bourgeoisie. The Jew reduced everything, he noted, including God, to the level of practical need. Their interests were exclusively material and money was their God. "Money is the jealous god of Israel before whom no other god may stand. Money debases all the gods of mankind and turns them into commodities . . . . The god of the Jews has been secularized and become the god of the world. Exchange is the true god of the Jew. His god is nothing more than illusory exchange."[3] These passages represent a theme which runs through Marx's writings, on the basis of which he has often been charged with anti-Semitism. There is undoubtedly some substance in the accusation, but the situation is more complex than might appear at first glance. In the first place, Marx was not the only person to suggest that something in Jews "took to" business and commerce and that they were indeed quite skillful at operating within a free market system. In fact, it was probably Moses Hess who first suggested to Marx the connection between religion, Judaism and economic alienation.[4] For a time, such statements incurred charges of bigotry but in this era of pluralism it should be possible to think in terms of group characteristics without being accused of harboring prejudice. Nor need one be a Marxist to see a correlation between Jews and free enterprise; some present-day Jewish neo-conservative thinkers argue along surprisingly similar lines. In the second place, we should notice Marx's claim that what we discover in Jewish commercial practice is "the secret of religion," and not just the Jewish religion. His critique is thus more universal.

Be that as it may, this strain in Marxist thought has engendered a degree of suspicion if not hostility among many scholars and articulators of Judaism. This has been exacerbated in recent years. Jewish thinkers have apparently assumed that they had little to learn from the "enemy" and they further supposed that they "knew" what the theoretical structures of that "enemy" were without submitting them to close scrutiny. The irony is that Marxism has exerted an indirect and "unnoticeable" influence on Jewish thought as one of the formative influences in the development of what might be called "sociological awareness": the recognition that the worlds of meaning and relationship that we inhabit are social, historical constructs and are affected by our material realities. Even the use, by theologians and others, of concepts such as "alienation," "ideology," and "determinism" owes something to the influence of the Marxist tradition, even though it may be difficult or impossible to specify that "something" with any precision. What I am suggestng, in other words, is that the influence of Judaism on Jewish affairs and Jewish life is still such, given the importance of the Middle East for example, as to render it dangerous for Jewish theology to be allowed to go about its business in real or imagined isolation from the forces that shape our culture, our intellectual traditions and our history and amongst these forces, Marxism certainly occupies a significant place.[5]

This encounter is particularly germane in the twentieth century, as Richard Rubenstein has noted. The peculiarities of our times is that although God is absent he is nevertheless rediscovered as the one "problem" which focuses the task of man, the crisis of thought and the dilemmas of time and history. Sartre may repudiate him with confidence, affirming "he is dead." He spoke to us and now is silent. Heidegger, with a calmness in striking contrast to the proclaiming zealot of Nietzsche's, may observe: "Because we hark back to Nietzsche's saying about the 'death of god,' people take such an enterprise

for atheism. For what is more logical than to consider the man
who has experienced the 'death of God' as a Godless person."
C. G. Jung, modifying the atheism of Sartre and the ontic
paganism of Heidegger, may make God a "function of the
unconscious" a projected reality which "does not exist
'absolutely,' that is independent of the human subject and
beyond all human conditions." Yet it is clear that the death of
God is but a metaphor for more profound death, for this God did
not die a natural death--he withered, contracted, starved to
death. He is no longer a constructive power in human existence,
he is among the displaced and unemployed. Not only are the
traditions of Judaism and Christianity discarded--this could be
tolerated, I suppose, for historic forms, to the extent that
they are merely historical, can be reviewed and amended. It is
rather that God as the Other, He who in His being is wholly
independent of the world and yet related to it as creator,
revealer, and redeemer, is dead. The death of God is the death
of the absolute. Henceforth each man is considered free to
authenticate his own existence according to Sartre, each man is
responsible for the rescue of Being according to Heidegger, each
man fashions his own God according to the deepest requirements
of his psyche, according to Jung.

There is a pathos in the concept of the "death of God" which
cannot be ignored. The 20th century--the century least able to
dispense with God--has, in fact, dispensed with God. It is
understandable for the 18th and 19th centuries to have abandoned
God--the enthusiasm of the Age of Enlightenment and the
complacent self-assurance of 19th century society could well
destroy religion. The 20th century, however, is the century of
tragedy, of genocide, of a threatening nuclear holocaust, the
century that has demonstrated what man can do if left to his own
desires. Unfortunately, it has become a post-religious century,
a century which has seen the end of religion. Rational religion
is gone; God is not a function of the mind, an object of
feeling, the foundation of ethics, the buttress of values and
standards. The conventional God may be dead. But Sartre and
Heidegger dispense not only with the God of convention and the
God of religon, they dispense with the God who is Absolute
Other. We find similar manifestations of theological despair in
the Jewish tradition occasioned by the shock of Auschwitz.

Because the Jewish God has always been a creative God of
history, Auschwitz destroyed for many Jews the faith in
history. YHWH acted at the Red Sea. He also acted at Sinai.

But Auschwitz too, is an historical event. Are the covenant and gas chambers dual aspects of the same God? How is it possible to reconcile the saving God of Abraham, Richard Rubenstein queries in After Auschwitz, with the God who was witness to the death of six million of His Chosen people? Were the Nazi murderers doing God's work? Unable to accept that possibility, Rubenstein resurrects the Lurianic God of nothingness who, having created the world and emptied Himself in this act of Tzimtzum, contraction, then withdrew from His object. After Auschwitz, the God of history is dead for Rubenstein, replaced by a God of absence, thus leaving temporal social existence devoid of divine encounter and intervention.[6]

Post-Holocaust Jewish thought was thus faced with a God who was inscrutable. God became a puzzlement and ambiguous, if not obnoxious; Jewish thought became heavy with despair. Classical Jewish thought and Jewish mysticism were optimistic, were generated by faith in an activist God and man who intervened and moved history. Post-Holocaust thought, in contrast, sank into anger and emptiness. It lost faith in history and could never trust the future again. Human action seemed helpless against the blind forces of fate. There was little that the individual could do and life was seen as being empty and tragic. The times may thus be ripe for a theological negotiation between Judaism and Marxism since Marxism, as Robert Tucker has argued, has as its core the "redemptive idea" that people can and will transform their history.[7]

It might be useful, at this point, for me to reflect briefly on the concepts and assumptions that I think are of essence in the Marxist intellectual tradition, particularly as they relate to what I believe is central in Judaism. It should be emphasized that Marxism is upheld here less as a doctrine than as a method.

In the Decameron, Boccaccio describes a Jew named Abraham who travels to Rome to examine at first hand the claims of Christianity. Finding corruption rampant in the Papal Court, Abraham thereupon converts to Christianity, reasoning that if the Christian religion survives and prospers despite the efforts of the clergy to destroy it, it must have divine support.

A 20th century Abraham would likely become a convert to Marxism. Marx's doctrines survive and flourish despite all that is done in his name. An apostle of liberation, Marx is invoked by admirers of Stalinist terror, and Marxism has given the world more than a half-dozen repressive and anti-libertarian regimes.

Marx was a militant atheist; there are religious Marxists. Marx was virulently anti-Zionist and anti-nationalist; there are Zionist Marxists. Marx was relentlessly rationalistic; there are existential Marxists and Freudian Marxists. Marx advocated action--praxis; there are pacifist Marxists. Marx despised, above all else, parliamentary liberalism; yet Western Europe is witnessing a boom in Parliamentary Marxism.

Why? Is there in Marx's teaching some elusive core of truth, some transcending historical value that enables it to flourish?

"A specter is haunting Europe--the specter of Communism. All the powers of old Europe have entered into a holy alliance to exorcise this specter: Pope and Czar, Metternich and Guizot, French Radicals and German police spies." It is now about 135 years since Karl Marx and Friederich Engels wrote that resounding first paragraph to the Communist Manifesto, and time can hardly be said to have dulled their words or to have relegated their ideas to the backburner of history. I want to emphasize again that I am not talking about the Soviet Union or the spectre of a worldwide Red Communist revolution. What I will be focusing on is Marxism as a way of looking at the world, as a social theory, as an intellectual tradition. To reject or ignore an important intellectual traditon of criticism, as much of contemporary Jewish thought seems to be doing, because of the Soviet Union, Cuba, or the P.L.O., for example, would be intellectual self-defeatism.

Now Marxism is an intellectual tradition, one of social analysis. The Greeks and Romans were asking one basic question--change. How do you explain physical change? Marxism asks a different question--how do you explain social and economic change? As such, Marxism is truly a modern political philosphy. It is one of the most important of the post-Industrial philosophies for it seeks to understand the structure of the contemporary world. And it has had a profound influence on how we view our world, whether we know it or not or whether we agree with it or not. Marx's essential theory which asserts that the most important question to be asked of any phenomenon is concerned with the relation which it bears to the economic structure, has created new tools of criticism and research whose use has altered the direction and emphasis of the social sciences in our generation. All those whose work rests on social observation are necessarily affected. Not only the conflicting classes and their leaders in every country, but historians and sociologists, psychologists and political scientists, critics and creative artists, so far as they try to analyze the changing quality of the life of their society, owe the form of their ideas in part to the work of Karl Marx and those laboring in his tradition. His thought was, and continues to be, revolutionary.[8]

Marx remained all of his life an oddly isolated figure among the revolutionaries of his time, hostile and opposed to their basic methods and their objectives. No matter how widely the majority of European democrats, utopians, even anarchists differed in character and aims, they basically agreed on two fundamental principles: that society was reformable and that it could be achieved by the determined will of individuals. Marx rejected both of these assumptions. He was convinced that human history is governed by laws which cannot be altered by the mere intervention of individuals and that change cannot be achieved from above by applying temporary structures to fundamental problems, but must be achieved through a total transformation of society, occasioned by the inevitable class struggle that Marx saw as the generating energy of history. It was therefore important for Marx to understand the nature and laws of the historical process, and that is why he spent thousands of hours pouring over documents in the British Museum which described with stark reality the industrial world of 19th century England. What he found in the documents and what he personally observed was a world in which working people lived in wretched homes; whole families, sometimes more than one family living in one room; relatives sleeping together, often without beds to sleep on; ill nourished on flour mixed with sawdust; poisoned by ptomaine from rancid meat; doping themselves and their wailing children with laudanum; spending their lives, without a sewage system, along the piles of their excrement and garbage; spreading epidemics of typhus and cholera. Marx needed to understand how an economic system could get this way. His theory of <u>historical materialism</u> provided the answer.

"The philosophers have only interpreted the world, in various ways; the point is to change it."[9] This eleventh "Thesis on Feuerbach," written in 1845, bears witness to a conviction already discernible in the "Paris Manuscripts" of 1844. In these manuscripts, we find Marx reflecting on man's alienation from the work of his hands, from his fellow men and from the world of nature. This insight was hardly innovative since it set him alongside Feuerbach and much of the complex tradition of post-Hegelian German philosophy. What was new was his claim that the contradictions in the human tradition demand resolution. Not a theoretical or philosophical resolution in thought, but rather a resolution in fact.

"Hitherto," Marx says in the opening words of The German Ideology, "men have always formed wrong ideas about themselves, about what they are and what they ought to be. They have arranged their relations according to their ideas of God, of normal man, etc. The products of their brains have got out of their hands. They, the creators, have bowed down before their creations. Let us liberate them from the chimeras, the ideas, dogmas, imaginary beings under the yoke of which they are pining away. Let us revolt against this rule of concepts."[10] It seems clear that this "liberation", this "revolt", must take the form of an inversion of the present state of reality: it must be such to allow people to arrange their ideas about "God" and of "normal man", according to their relationships, rather than the other way around. In this way, people will be liberated from the idols they have made; idols which stand over against them as alien and alienating powers.

If the goal is truth and freedom, Marx urged that we avoid the illusions of "the German ideology". Our focus must not be on ideas, but on people, on their activities in the material conditions of their lives. "All historical writing must set out from these natural bases and their modification in the course of history through the action of man."[11] And the history of the "modification" of nature by human action is the history of the modes of production.

In these ideas Marx is laying down two fundamental features of what he will call "historical materialism". The first, which is one of the most important concepts in Marxism, is that man produces himself through labor, through physically and mentally "working" the conditions of his existence. The second is the insistence that, if we pay attention to "real individuals", to what they produce with their hands and minds, and to the modes of production, then we must proceed historically, or else we will find ourselves suffering from the illusion that contemporary modes of production are timeless and immutable. Materialist method is thus historical method or, better put, historical method is a matter of perceiving the process of human action in the material world.

History, for Marx, is thus the struggle of people to realize their full human potentialities. Man's effort to fully realize himself is a struggle to escape from being the plaything of forces that seem capricious and arbitrary, that is, to attain mastery of them and of himself, which is the state of feedom. People attain this subjugation of the world not by an increase in knowledge obtained by thinking as Aristotle had supposed--but by the activity of labor--the conscious moulding by people of their environment and each other--the essential unity of theory and praxis. Labor transforms the world and the individual himself, too, in the process of the activity. The history of society is the history of the inventive labors that change people, alter their habits, outlooks, relationships to other men and to nature. Among man's inventions--conscious or unconscious--is the division of labor which increases the possibility of productivity, thus creating wealth beyond our immediate needs. This accumulation in its turn creates the possibility of leisure and culture; but also the abuse of this surplus by those who have, to coerce and exploit those who don't, thereby dividing people into classes--the controllers and controlled. History, for Marx, is the interaction between the lives of these two actors on the human stage. The complex web can only be understood and controlled if the central dynamic factor responsible for the direction of the process is grasped. For Marx that generating factor is the class struggle. The character of the age in which Marx lived was, in his view, determined by this class war; the behavior and outlook of individuals and societies was determined by this factor--this was the central historical truth of a culture, anticipated by Defoe's Crusoe, which relies on accumulation and by the battles to control this accumulation. But precisely because it is an historical predicament, it was not eternal. Nothing is eternal--history moves, history transforms itself. The only permanent factor in the history of humankind is people themselves, intelligible only in terms of the struggle which is part of their essence, the struggle to master nature and organize their productive powers in a rational fashion. Work, in the cosmic vision of Marx, is what makes men and their relationships what they are; its distortion by the division of labor and the class war leads to degradation, dehumanization, exploitative human relationships, and conscious and unconscious falsifications of vision to conceal this reality. When this has been understood, and action, which is the concrete expression of such understanding takes place, instead of dividing and enslaving people, unites and liberates them: gives full expression to their creative capacities in the only form in which human nature is wholly free--in common endeavor, social cooperation, etc.

So for Marx, what gave its specific character to any given society was the system of economic relations which governed that society. In a much celebrated passage, he summarized this view as follows:

> "In the social production which men carry on, they enter into definite relations that are indispensable and independent of their will; these relations of production correspond to a definite stage of development of their material powers of production. The sum total of these productive relations constitutes the economic structure of society--the real foundation on which rise legal and political superstructures, and to which correspond definite forms of social consciousness . . . It is not the consciousness of men that determines their existence, but on the contrary their social existence determines their consciousness. At a certain stage of their development, the material forces of production in society come into conflict with the existing relations of production--with the property relations within which they had been at work before. From forms of development of the productive forces these relations turn into their fetters. Then comes the period of social revolution with the change of the economic foundation the whole vast superstructure is sooner or later entirely transformed . . . . No social order ever disappears before all the productive forces, for which there is room in it, have developed, and the new higher relations of production never appear before the conditions of their existence have matured in the wound of the old society . . . , the problem itself only arises when the material conditions necessary for its solution already exist or are at least in the process of formation."[12]

Marx's use of the image of birth invites us to see the entire process of human existence, past and present, not merely as the history of society, but as a prolonged and often agonizing process of gestation: as the process of man's prehistory. And he says precisely this: "The bourgeois mode of production is the last antagonistic form of the social process of production . . . . The prehistory of human society accordingly closes with this social formation."[13] All history before the emergence of communism is "prehistory" for Marx since it is not yet the human history of man. There is in this notion an element of eschatological prophecy not unrelated to Jewish Messianism, which may have been born with the destruction of the Second Temple or may already be inherent in the Genesis account of Creation.

It is not only that Marx's language concerning the "birth" of humanity from the revolutionary overthrow of capitalism announces a state of affairs in which human existence will be "redeemed," in which man's alienation will be healed, that justifies the description of such language as eschatological. It is, rather, Marx's apparent conviction that once achieved, this state of affairs will be irreversible. Whatever changes and modifications individual existence and social organization may experience after the post-revolutionary "birth" of mankind from "prehistory," these changes will not carry the risk of reversal or the re-emergence of class struggle. Conflictual "prehistory" is over and human history begins. This conviction indicates the presence of an eschatological element in his thought.

For Marx, no less than for the anarchists, people are potentially wise, creative and free. If their character has deteriorated beyond recognition, that is due to the long and brutalizing class wars and exploitation in which they and their ancestors have lived ever since society ceased to be that primitive communism out of which it has developed. However, Marx is the eternal optimist. History has been moving in an inexorable, progressive fashion. The gradual freeing of mankind has pursued a definite, irreversible direction: every new epoch is inaugurated by the liberation of a heretofore oppressed class; nor can a class, once it has been eliminated, ever return. History does not move backwards, or in cyclical movements: it moves straight ahead and forward. A knowledge, a consciousness of this process is essential to effective political action. Implicit here is the notion that people can, people must act, must participate in their own liberation. So the ancient world gave way to the medieval, slavery to feudalism and feudalism to the industrial bourgeoise. Each of these changes was an improvement.

And now only one stratum remains submerged below the level of the rest, one class remains enslaved, the landless, propertyless proletariat, created by the advance of technology and industry. The proletariat is on the lowest possible rung of the social scale: there is no class below it; by securing its own emacipation the proletariat will therefore emancipate mankind. It has, unlike other classes, no specific claim, no interest of its own which it does not share with all people as such: for it has been stripped of everything but its bare humanity--what it is entitled to, is the minimum to which all people are entitled to. Its fight is thus not for one class, but for the natural rights of all. And while history is determined and the victory will ultimately be won, how rapidly this will occur, how efficiently, how far in accordance with the popular will, depends on human initiative, on the degree of understanding of their task by the masses.

Such, briefly summarized, is the theory of history and society which constitutes the metaphysical basis of Marxism, of the preconditions of that definitive, unsurpassable and eschatological transformation of human society which he sees as implicit in the logic of the development of capitalism. What will be the outcome or aftermath of such a revolution, Marx does not disclose. He is in the business not of predicting the future, but of analyzing current trends. It is by no means a wholly empirical theory, since it does not confine itself to an empirical description of any pehnomenon and the formulation of a hypothesis based on this data. Often the data is bent to fit the theory. The Marxist doctrine of movement in dialectical collisions--change comes through clash of opposites--is not a hypothesis wedded to particular facts, but a pattern, uncoverd by a non-empirical, historical method, a historical hunch, so to speak, the validity of which is never questioned.

Why is the theory so impressive, then? In the sharpness and clarity with which this theory formulates its questions, in the rigor of the method by which it proposes to search for the answers, in its passion to critique, in the combination of attention to detail and power of wide comprehensive generalization, it is without parallel. Even if all its specific conclusions were proved false, its importance in creating a wholly new attitude to social and historical questons, and so opening new avenues of human knowledge, would be unimpaired. He set out to and did refute the proposition that ideas or religion decisively determine the course of history. He replaced this with the scientific study of historically evolving economic relations and of their bearing on other aspects of the lives of communities and individuals. If nothing else occurred, this would be a revolutionary achievement.

Now Marx's philosophy, like much of existentialist thinking, represents a protest against man's alienation, his loss of his identity and his transformation into an object, his reification; essentially it is a movement against the dehumanization and automatization of man inherent in the development of Western industrialism. In this sense, Marx's philosophy is very much rooted in the Western humanist philosophical tradition; it may even be seen as part of the prophetic Judeo-Christian tradition because at its essence, when you parce away the economic materialism, is a concern for man and the realization of his potentialities.

It is clear, then, that an anthropology, a conception of the essence of nature of humanity, occupied a central place in Marx's thought. According to this conception, the essence of man is to be found in work, sociability and consciousness.

The central issue is that of the existence of the "real" individual, who is what he does, in other words, whose life is an extension of his work, and who is defined and shaped by his society. One of Marx's greatest insights, as has already been emphasized, is that he sees man in his full development as a member of a given society and of a given class; aided in his development by his society and class, but at the same time its captive. For that higher form of society to be realized, it is essential that not only our alienation from the process and products of our labor be overcome, but also our alienation from ourselves and from our fellow human beings. It is, in other words, a necessary condition of the emancipation of the world that human beings achieve self-mastery. And such self-mastery is not to be construed in purely individualistic terms: it must refer to the emergence of a society which is free from the external alienating forces, be they class, state or idea.[14]

Now there is a great deal of misunderstanding and misreading of Marx. Because much of Marx's writings deal with matters economic, with "materialism," Marx is supposed to have believed that the paramount psychological motive in people is their wish for material gain and comfort. Complementary to this idea is the equally widespread assumption that Marx neglected the importance of the individual; that he had neither respect nor understanding for the spiritual needs of man. This view of Marx then goes on to discuss his socialist paradise as one of millions of people who submit to an all-powerful state bureaucracy, people who have surrendered their freedom and their individuality.

This view of Marx's materialism, his anti-spiritual tendency, his wish for uniformity, is incorrect. Marx's aim was to liberate the individual from the pressure of economic needs, so that he can be fully human; his aim was that of the spiritual emancipation of man, of his liberation from the chains of economic determination; of reconstituting him in his human

wholeness, of enabling him to find unity and harmony with his
fellow man and with nature. And this would only make sense once
we had liberated ourselves from subsistence.

Marx's concept of socialism follows from his concept of the
individual. It should be clear by now that according to this
concept, socialism is not a society of regimented, automatized
individuals. It is not a society in which the individual is
subordinated to the state. Instead the aim of socialism is
people; it is to free people. It is to create a form of
production and an organization of society in which people can
overcome alienation from their product, from their work, from
their fellow man, from themselves and from nature. In a
socialist society, people produce in an associated,
non-competitive way; they produce rationally and in an
unalienated way, which means that they bring production under
their control, instead of being ruled by it. Marx expected that
by this form of an unalienated society man would become
independent, stand on his own feet; that he would truly be the
master and creator of his life and hence that he could begin to
make living his main business, rather than producing the means
for a living.

Does not all this mean that Marx's socialism is in a
fundamental way the realization of the deepest religious
impulses in man? Is not his concern for the individual a deeply
felt non-theistic kind of religion? This is how I read Marx and
in this sense he is very much a modern extension of the
prophetic, messianic impulse.[15] The prophets of the Old
Testament, of the Tanach are not only spiritual leaders, they
are also political leaders. They not only describe what they
see, but give a vision of how things should be--a normative
perspective. The Hebrew prophets share the idea that history is
important, that people perfect themselves in the process of
history, and that they will eventually create a social order of
peace and justice. Man lives in the world and salvation, for
the prophets, begins in the here and now, not in a state of
transcending history. This means that man's spiritual aims are
inseparably connected with the transformation of society;
politics is basically not a realm that can be divorced from that
of moral values and of man's self-realization. Marx and
socialism are very much part of this tradition. It took history
seriously, it was optimistic about social change and it returned
to the idea of the "good society" as the condition for the
realization of man's spiritual needs.

The Marxist notion of praxis, of critical activity, is consonant with the prophetic ideas of human participation in creation, in the redemptive quality of human action. In addition, the Marxist commitment to historicity, to future, to societal tranformation, corresponds to the prophetic faith in history. Lastly, the conceptions of objectification, of action, which are so central to Marxist ethics, overlap and cohere to the prophetic notion of human decision, of the individual who must act because human deed is a necessary component of Divine action. These ideas are not alien to certain intellectual and theological traditions within Judaism.

Classical Jewish theology and Jewish mysticism abound in ideas that can act as a bridge between Judaism and Marxism.

Now what is central in Judaism? The most obvious answer is the Torah. The Torah is God's drama--the blueprint of a moral world waiting to be realized. Judaism is Torah--"teaching." The Aramaic Targum correctly translates it Oraita, while the Greek Septuagint incorrectly renders it nomos--law. Torah is more than law, it is a rule of life for all people, a pattern of behavior, a "direction" revealed in the life of a people through prophets and sages, which if properly followed, leads to the well-being of the individual and of society. The term Halachah which the Rabbis employed for laws based on the Torah, means the proper way in which an individual should walk. "The Lord will establish you as His holy people . . . if you keep the mizvot of the Lord your God and walk in His ways" (Deut. 28:9). Judaism's "way" is designed to sustain and advance life, not to escape or transcend it. Rabbinic Judaism elucidates this principle.

> R. Hama . . . said: What does the text mean: you shall walk after the Lord your God? . . . The meaning is to walk after the attributes of the Holy One, blessed be He. As He clothes the naked . . . so do you . . . clothe the naked; as the Holy One, blessed be He, visits the sick, . . . so do you visit the sick; as the Holy One, blessed be He, comforts mourners, . . . so do you comfort mourners; as the Holy One, blessed be He, buries the dead, so do you bury the dead. (Sotah 14a)

Its roots are set deep in the practical needs of man and it is fully responsive both to his instincts and his highest aspirations. So the Torah is God's play and the physical world with its necessary imperfections, is the stage on which the drama will unfold. This world--existence, reality, matter, pain, enjoyment--is, in a poetic sense, a divine necessity. It is the raw material through which the creative urge is satisfied and finds form. Life is good and a gracious gift of God. One should not experience any sense of guilt in the legitimate enjoyments of life. They are of God. Man must worship God with his entire being--with body, mind and soul.[16]

This drama implies that God, although free from the physical limitations of time and space, nevertheless acts as if motivated by a spiritual need, by a need to realize a moral order. It implies that God who is free from the limitations of the world, is nevertheless limited in a Heschelian and Buberian sense, in his dependence on a human partner, the actual builder of the moral world. God does need man for His fulfillment; the I-Thou divine dialogical relationship is a two-way street. To use the superb imagery of Judah Halevi, "When I go forth to seek Thee, I find Thee seeking me."

There are dangers in this situation. For man to be a partner, he must be free. But freedom without the potential of rebellion, sin, even the ultimate evil of an Auschwitz, is no freedom at all. Evil may destroy creation and the possibility of partnership. However, the inner dialectic of God's plan requires a free human being, armed with intelligence and the potential of becoming evil. A computer devoid of impulses, a being like the angels, would lack the capacity to create. The Bible contains this principle in the notion of Hester Panim (The Hiding Face of God): the view that at times God, mysteriously and inexplicably, hides from man, that God's hiddenness is required for man to be a moral creature. God's hiddenness allows man free will. God has to abstain from interfering if human action is to possess value. Unfortunately, it is this very creative factor that often subverts the plan.

According to the Talmud, God was well aware of this difficulty: He was torn between his desire to realize the Torah and His knowledge that a man armed with freedom could create chaos and destroy the world. But in an act of divine "bravery" He created man.[17]

In the basic thought of Judaism then, good and evil are not cosmic forces in eternal conflict, wherein one must destroy the other. Judaism rejects Manichaean dualism. They are complementary attributes of God's creation, which are reconciled through a living Torah.

Like some volatile chemicals before adequate preparation, the yetzer haRah in its raw state is dangerous and potentially explosive. However, when processed by the Torah and sublimated by the rationality of the law, it becomes a vital and indispensable element in human life--the very impetus of the

world of creation.[18] As energy in the raw, it destroys;
structured and chanelled, it creates. Once man becomes aware of
his epistemological nakedness, God Himself must help him to
fashion a cenceptual garment. The Torah is that conceptual
garment.

Law, Halachah, is essentially a limit and boundry. Our
biological being is subject to the laws of nature and the law of
death; our intellectual grasp is restricted by the limitations
of our cognitive abilities. Religions of radical mysticism
rebel against these limits and in their hubris, create
intellectual Towers of Babel to storm the heights of the
spirit. By Gnosis, knowledge, reason, man can transcend his
biological finiteness, become one with the spirit and achieve
immortality, in short, become like the gods.

Judaism is not a religion of radical mysticism but one of
law and limit. God created the world with these limitations;
man must comply with them whether he understands the reasons or
not. He may, like Maimonides and others, try to rationalize the
Halachah, but he must approach any reform with great care. This
has appeared to many philosophers and social critics as an
expression of spiritual bondage; this has induced many to accuse
the Pharisees, the representative teachers of Judaism, of a lack
of individualism and extreme subjection to the rule of law, but
it is the necessary consequence and intrinsically consistent
form of historical Judaism. The religious Jewish experience is
a vital, unique, process-phenomenon involving the very essence
of being, the very meaning of existence. It implicates God and
a people of individuals committed to act out the convenantal
relationship. The awareness of God's word, the Torah, and
action denote a transformation of the self. To the moment when
God is present, the Jew responds with a specific conduct, a way
of being, a Halachah that translates into action the encounter
with God. That constitutes praxis: the individual's and
communities' committed actualization of God's word and religious
experience into prayer, ritual, customs and ethical action.
Praxis is the living experience of God.

In cultures where man thought that he could become like a
god, knowledge--either in the form of a secret gnosis or a
philosophical discipline--was often considered as the key to
eternal life: Gilgamesh comes to Utnapishtim and individuals
joined mystery religions--all in search of knowledge which made
men like gods, immortal.[19] Our current fascination with the
redeeming possibilities of science and technology, what T. S.

Eliot described as the effort "to devise the perfect refrigerator and work out a rational morality," are in the same spirit. It is the hypostatization, the reification of knowledge and reason. Systems of thought and technological innovations and the toys that they create for us comprise the new idolatry of the age. Marx, of course, was very sensitive to this trap. He insisted that there is no "pure" consciousness, pure thought. They are affected by the material conditions of society, as in language. "Language itself is the product of a community, just as it is in another respect itself the presence of the community."[20] It follows that, if the community is, in fact, rent with class divisions, structures of domination and alienation, then the language or languages in which the community expresses itself will be similarly distorted. The users of language, however, are commonly unable to perceive its distortions. Hence the folly of those philosophers who imagine that one can "think" change into existence. However, in Judaism, where the gap between man and God is ultimate, absolute, nothing--not even knowledge and study which are venerated in the tradition--can bring about such a transformation. As long as Judaic man accepts the authority of God, he is forced to make peace with the limitations of his mind, not for the purpose of being like God, but simply to listen to His commands and to live justly and humanely in an imprefect world.

Where there is no belief in the reality of progress, there is no summons to social action. One finds a mature, philosophical concept of ethics among the best classical writers, but there is no passion for justice among them, no activist urge to improve the social and economic conditions of life of whose inhumanity they were fully aware. In Judaism we find this passion to improve the world, we find this social revolutionary ethic. Judaism has always concerned itself with social change. Every religion that projects a vision of a better world in the manner in which Prophetic Judaism does, will always be critical of existing conditions. It is not enough to know what justice is: one must seek justice. "Zedek, Zedek Tirdof--Justice, Justice you shall pursue," the Deuteronomist proclaims. It is not enough to know truth; one must "seek truth," Jeremiah emplores. Judaism, because it is a this-worldly religion, preached social progress as a reality, as necessary, and as the supreme challenge and mitzvah. This is the very meaning and essence of Judaic prophecy. Judaism did not approve of a spiritual egocentrism which sought fulfillment not in humanity and social enterprise but in a detached salvationism, non-action or other-worldliness. It demanded inner change, of course, but it did not lightly dismiss the social imperatives. In matchless eloquence the prophets of Israel called upon men and women to think less of their rituals, and more of the weak and wronged in their midst, the disfranchised and the oppressed. They talked of the world as in the process of becoming, of creation as an ongoing process with humankind having the responsibility for its completion. They urged people to believe that society can be improved if they will just act. The good society can be built here on earth, free from war, from exploitation, from fear (Is. 2:1-4; Mic. 4:104).

The Messianic hope of a this-worldly revolution is, indeed, a feature unique in occidental thought. The Hebrew prophets of the Tanach are not only spiritual leaders; they are political leaders. They not only describe and critique the world as they see it, but they show humankind a prescriptive version of how it ought to be. They share the idea that history must be taken seriously, that it has a meaning, that it is in constant motion, that humanity realizes and perfects itself in the process of history, and that through its actions, it will eventually create a social order of equality and justice. In the Jewish Bible, God is revealed in history as a creative actor ("the God of Abraham, the God of Isaac, the God of Jacob"), and in history, not in a state of transcending history, lies the salvation of man. This means that humanity's spiritual aims are inseparably connected with the transformation of society; politics is not a realm that can be divorced from spiritual values and humanity's self-actualization.

The doctrine of redemption in Judaism thus proclaims the transcendence of man's alienation from God, from nature, and from his fellow-man. To the extent that man is alienated from nature, from his work, his humanity and his fellow human beings, he is thereby alienated from God. It makes no sense to speak of man at peace with God and in enmity with man. Nor does it make sense to speak of man estranged from God and reconciled with his humanity and his fellow human beings. If the Marxian moral protest is registered in the name of a conception of the human, of non-alienation and the threatened process of seeking to critically understand the historical circumstances of its occurence, the Jewish moral protest is, or should be, registered in the name of a conception of the human derived from the practical process of the following of the Halachah, and the theoretical process of seeking critically to interpret the history of sin and redemption in the light of the Torah.

To a varying degree, the Jews of modernity are still heir to this tradition. Secularism has clearly made substantial inroads and today there is no normative religious expression of Judaism accepted by the entire community. Nonetheless, there is an important continuity evinced in Jewish attitudes towards politics. Jews continue to insist that reality match up to ideals of social justice and human fellowship. Such was the case for the Hebrew Prophets, but also for the Jewish Marxists, for Bundists in Czarist Russia and Jewish members of the "New Left" in the 1960s, those associated with Breira in the 1970s and New Jewish Agenda in the 1980s. Thus it can fairly be maintained that one attitude which is distinctly non-Jewish is the complacent acceptance of stasis, the willingness to countenance injustice or even the status quo for the sake of quiet security. Ernest Renan was correct; Jews possess "a thirst for the future."

Judaism was thus never induced by despair to succumb to the religious perspective which regarded human life as evil. Judaism, certainly in its Rabbinic formulation, did have a doctrine of immortality, but it took the form of a resurrection of the body not of an escape of the soul from the prison of the body to live in another world. Believing that the human body is the creation of God, not of some evil Gnostic Demiourgos, the Jews could not detach themselves from earthly existence. This is fundamental to Judaism and accounts for its continual concern to develop a halachah, a law to cope with the exigencies of ordinary human life. This too is the basic reason why Jews could not give up their communal ideal and accept enslavement, be it spiritual or political.

Judaism thus did not shun the world; it was committed to living in it with a passionate attachment to social progress. "The Hebrew Bible," writes Abraham Joshua Heschel, "is not a book about heaven—it is a book about the earth. The Hebrew word, eretz, meaning 'land,' occurs at least five times as often in the Bible as the word shamayim, meaning 'heaven.'" Rabbi Kook, the mystic and late Chief Rabbi of Israel, defined the essence of Judaism in terms of an existentialist philosphy which minimized dogmatic affirmations or ritual practices. For him the essence of Judaism which flows from Jewish monotheism is the passion to overcome the separatism which severs man from nature, from his fellow man, and from God. It is the passion to perfect the world through man's awareness of his links to all else in existence. It is the rejection of the alleged antagonism between the material and the spiritual. It is the rejection of naturalism as an ultimate center of moral values. "The Jewish outlook," he says, "is the vision of the holiness of all existence."[21] The world is not to be escaped from nor exploited; it is to be shaped, transformed and experienced even with all its shortcomings and evils, utilizing the insights of the Torah. The accent, however, is on a socially meaningful project.

**

The Jewish concept of Messianism was also infused with this worldly, historical considerations. For Judaism, salvation traditionally is a physical not a purely spiritual concept. The Messianic age, to the Jews, is to be the culmination of human history on earth. Even the world to come, to the extent that it was described by the Rabbis, is to take place on earth, and the rebirth of the righteous is to be a resurrection of not only the body but the body politic in an earthly paradise--not a ethereal Heaven.

There is less individualism in the Jewish concept of the Messiah than in the Christian concept. While the Christian concept centers around the person of the Messiah--Christ who descends from an extra-historical dimension to save the believer, the Jewish Messiah represents an era rather than a person; he is the culmination of a particular stage in historical development. This messianic perspective arose out of monotheism.

Jewish monotheism unified human history into a cohesive process moving inexorably towards one final aim, the fulfillment of God's purposes on earth. Monotheism also carried with it a revolutionary social message. Since all people were created by the One God, all people were brothers. Monotheism began as a religion determined not to submit to any oppressive individual or class. It outlawed the cult of the god-priest-king. It stressed the concern of the one God for each individual, without intermediary, priests, demigods or gods; and one of its chief preoccupations was social justice. Polytheism, in contrast, provided no such progressive historical drama. Each nation had its own deities and there was no overriding purpose for mankind. History was regarded as cyclic. Judaism, however, claimed to be in contact with a supreme being who was not indifferent to humanity and who moulded the process of history. This concept of progress in history towards a final Utopia, be it spiritual or secular, has been the innovation of the progressive and utopian traditions in Western culture. We see this in Marxism's emphasis of the proletariat's messianic vocation. The proletariat is the new Israel, history's chosen people, the liberator and builder of an earthly kingdom that is to come. Marxism's proletarian communism is a secularized form of the ancient Jewish chiliasm. A chosen class takes the place of a chosen people.

In addition to these trends in classical Judaism, there exists a body of modern Jewish literature and thought which has also remained true to the prophetic and mystical traditions of Jewish culture and which incorporates such major themes as a hope, openness to future, historical fulfillment, immanence, the potentiality of human praxis, and the value of Being. This body of Jewish literature not only escaped the cultural pessimism and negation-of-history of most contemporary Jewish discourse, but it also offers a bridge, an opening for a Jewish-Marxist dialogue. To repeat, the question here is not about the existence or non-existence of God. The question posed here does not concern the deeper loyalty to Party or to Synagogue. The question before us is the contemporary wasteland. The problem them becomes to find a common conceptual armory, to find notions and themes which are shared by both Jews and Marxists, so that they can join and ally in the process of transcendence, be it secular or spiritual.

Influenced by European existentialism, Franz Rosenzweig, the German-Jewish philosopher, concentrated upon the notions of creation, creation anew, human involvement in creation anew.[22] It was Rosenzweig who first made clear that the ancient faith of Israel was not just compatible with the externals of modern culture, but that Judaism was in fact the only answer to the deepest problems of the Jew's existence in the contemporary world. His magnum opus, The Star of Redemption (Der Stern der Erloesung) written during his service as an Unteroffizcer in World War One on postcards and scraps of paper and sent to his mother for transcription, delineates the basis of his religious outlook. He argued that a meaningful religion required more than commandments, more even than ethical action. It required existential thinking that would aid man to understand his purpose. In order to achieve this understanding one needed faith in God's design. For Rosenzweig such faith could not be other than a divine-human encounter, a dialogue where both spheres interact with each other. Rosenzweig's God is not a remote lawgiver, not a mere synonym for a moral idea. It is a God who actually enters into one's life at every point and thereby gives life meaning. Rosenzweig was convinced that he divined the three basic ideas of Judaism: Creation, Revelation, and Redemption. By accepting these ideas--and their ritual requirements--one brought God into one's daily circuit and communicated with Him. This dialogue prevented religious observance from becoming an uninspired routine. Indebted to Nietzsche, Rosenzweig pictures a world which is ever being created anew, and calls upon man to say yes, to affirm, and to participate in this ongoing process. For Rosenzweig, the world is unfinished. It is Becoming, Eternal Becoming. Man, the Yes-Sayer must collaborate and participate in this ongoing and continuous creation. The role of man is vital: human praxis plays a central, pivotal role in Rosenzweig's thought. Human action is an indispensable component of historical fulfillment. Rosenzweig's conception is essentially historical. Creation is the enduring base of things; that is, history as process is the primal factum of existence. But Rosenzweig welcomes this historicity. It means that the unfinished world requires man to complete it.

Creation is given, the locus of man is defined, the ambit of his acts is described; however, at the heart of Judaism is the insistence that the future is still open. What remains open--what forms the giveness of the beginning to the indefinite but confident expectation of the end--is what Rosenzweig calls "the eternal task" of man. What concerns Rosenzweig is that man should achieve not precision in understanding but sublime involvement in the work of creation and redemption. Theology is therefore restricted by him to pedagogy. A concept is useful only if it instructs life, a doctrine is valuable only if it functions in the ordering of human ends. Judaism is never a problem; but it is always a task.

Rosenzweig's anthropology is dignified, is Promethean. Reflecting the tones of Marx, Rosenzweig speaks of man as something which moved beyond himself, as self-transcendent. In his essay, "Understanding the Sick and the Healthy," Rosenzweig identifies man as one who signifies. Man is a creature who gives names. In short, man is the being who gives meaning to the world around him. Truth does not exist, but man brings

truth into existence. History does not exist, but man brings
history into the future. Rosenzweig not only testifies to the
activity, but also to the fact that man has brought
signification to existence. Man is the generative principle.
Rosenzweig conducted an anthropocentric revolution: he made man
the center, the axis of history.

Rosenzweig devoted his short life to a sustained effort to
thus appropriate Judaism existentially. In the process, he
pointed to a new conception of Judaism, transcending the
opposition between the fundamentalism of much of Orthodox Jewish
thought on the one hand, and the rationalism and humanism of
many Liberal and Reform Jewish positions on the other, around
which much of Jewish religious discussion in the nineteenth and
twentieth centuries revolved. Rosenzweig did not share the
Orthodox view that the traditional 613 Mitzvot are the eternal
laws of God. The Halakhah, in his view, was not meant to be
unchanging; it was to be a living, growing process. Orthodoxy
had erred in congealing the halakhah into the fixed paragraphs
of Caro's Shulchan Aruch (prepared table). For the Jew of
today, Rosenzweig urged, observance of the traditional law must
become a personal, existential, freely chosen act. The Mitzvot
must be made to live, must be felt as personally addressed to
the individual. For this to occur each Jew must intelligently
choose, must discover which precepts of the Halakhah he is able
to fulfill.[23]

Hence Rosenzweig's initiation of a new approach to Jewish
learning. With the help of Rabbi Nehemiah A. Nobel, the
Orthodox communal Rabbi of Frankfurt, Rosenzweig succeeded in
establishing in 1919 the Freie Judische Lehrhaus, a unique
institution for adult Jewish studies where the teachers and
students would together explore the major sources of Judaism and
through free and open discussion seek to learn from them how to
be Jews in the modern world. Here Rosenzweig advocated a
reorientation in Judaism to result from re-established contact
with the original sources and from renewed practice of Judaism.
The basic attitude is freedom. No laws can be proclaimed, no
rules can be set. But the sincere attempt, he hoped, could not
fail in restoring the religious quality to Jewish learning and
living. This was not a forlorn dream.

In 1922, at the very height of his career, Rosenzweig was
stricken with an agonizing disease, creeping lateral sclerosis,
which progressively paralyzed almost every part of his body.
Such was the spirit of this remarkable man, however, that the

eight years that remained to him were the years in which he
completed the most original of his essays. He sat strapped in
his chair, his neck supported by a pulley, using an especially
constructed typewriter; all the while his wife served as his
secretary. When he died in 1929 at the age of forty-three, he
bequeathed a personal religion of faith and reason that could be
accepted by the Jewish masses.

There were, in fact, thousands of Jews who were searching
for a way to return to traditional faith and who were attracted
by this "revelation." Because the emphasis of the Lehrhaus
concept was not outward from the Torah, but inward from life, it
exerted a major influence on the semi-assimilated German-Jewish
community. Rosenzweig, through the institution and his works,
demonstrated how one could affirm the authentic supernatural
religion of Judaism without falling into obscurantism, how one
could lead a Torah-true life without falling into legalism and
superstition. What Rosenzweig fought against with every fiber
in his being was the routinization, the secularization, the
sentimentalization of Judaism. On this ground he opposed
Orthodox fundamentalism; on this ground he opposed modernism.
And he was able to bequeath a personal religion of faith and
reason that could be accepted on its own theological terms
without reference to Jewish history, peoplehood, or sentimental
loyalties. He--along with his slightly older colleague Martin
Buber--showed that the ancient faith of prophets and Rabbis was
not merely compatible with the externals of modern culture, but
was in fact the answer to the deepest problems of existence in
contemporary society.[24]

We see a similar interest in the power of signification in
the great German literary critic, Walter Benjamin. Benjamin is
an interesting personality to focus on because he moved between
and had intellectual affinities to both traditions, Judaism and
Marxism.[25] In terms of this problem of signification, he was
primarily a metaphysician of language engaged in mystical
linguistics. Benjamin's theory of language can also serve as a
bridge between Judaism and Marxism. Benjamin, like the
Kabbalists, believed that language in itself is a form of
powerful action: "I do not believe that the word stands
somewhere farther away from the divine than does 'real'
action." He argued against Martin Buber that there is no sphere
of experience which is ineffable: the true task of language, he
wrote, using a kabbalistic imagery, is "the crystal-clear
elimination of the unsayable in language. Only where this

sphere of the wordless in its ineffable pure power is opened up, can the magic sparks spring between word and . . . act . . . Only the intensive directing of the words into the kernel of the innermost silence will achieve true action." Against Buber's mystical depreciation of language, Benjamin proposed a mystical theory in which language itself becomes an action: to speak is to make, is to create.

Benjamin added a theological dimension to his philosophy of language. In an early essay he deals with the question of how divine language can become human. God's word is equivalent to existence, but God could not have created the world by calling it directly into existence with concrete words, since God's language, by definiton, is undifferentiated and infinite. Because Divine language seems incommensurable with human language, Benjamin felt that an immediate, linguistic relationship between God and the world, Buber's "unmediated word of God," is impossible. Creation and, in fact, all interaction between God and the world must be mediated by man. God is the source of language, but it is man who names objects and thereby "brings the world before God." When man names, therefore, he repeats the process of creation and reestablishes the relationship between language and objects. This mystical linguistics obviously reflected Benjamin's view that man and his actions are at the center of the historical process responsible for interpreting and creating events. Without this theological belief in God as the source of language and in language as the mediation tool between the mind, essential reality and action, the work of interpretation is meaningless. Hence Benjamin saw interpretation of which translation is a special case, as in some ways the epitome of the creative process.[26] This notion of a divine language of names which underlies conventional language is very close to the Kabbalah's theory of the divine names as meaningless but meaning-bestowing.

It is in fact in the Zoharic tradition of the Kabbalah that we find within Judaism an articulation and celebration of the role of the individual in history which, conceptually, can provide a structure for the conversation, the bridge, between Judaism and Marxism that I am arguing for. The Zohar, the principle Kabbalistic text written at the end of the 13th century, represents a radical shift in Judaism's thinking about man and praxis. For according to the Zohar, God's relationship with the world is patterned on the model of a continuous flow of energy. God generates the energy, but it is man who must act like a prism, focusing and returning the energy to God. This energy, then, is renewed and returned to man who again focuses and returns it to God, and so on. It is an elliptical process having two aspects. God does not act independently and unilaterally of man. They each stand in a reciprocal relationship, each benefiting the other, each doing something that allows the other to achieve full existence.

What we have before us is a very powerful, and in some ways new insight into the nature of the man-God relationship, for the Zohar teaches that God is actually dependent upon man. It argues that God, having committed himself to creation, now needs man to complete it. This insight is revolutionary in its implications because more than ever before in Jewish thought, the individual is the active agent in the world. It is man who is responsible for the balance of forces in God. It is man who is responsible for the flow of Divine energy in God and in the world. As God becomes more dependent upon man, man becomes more responsible and powerful, not only for his own welfare, but for Messianic and historical restoration. Later Zoharic tradition increased even further the importance of man in the divine economy in the Lurianic movement with its myth of tsimtsum (the self-limitation of God), shevirat Hakelim (the shattering of the vessels) and tikkun (the restoration of the Cosmos and God to the primordial unity!).[27]

From the small town of Safed, in the upper Galilee, there emerged a revolution in Jewish mystical thought in the early sixteenth century associated with the name of Isaac Luria. Lurianic Kabbalism developed the concepts mentioned above. Tsimtsum means contraction or withdrawal. It means that the existence of the universe is made possible by a process of shrinkage in God. Luria explains the phenomenon by posing a question: How can there be a universe if God is everywhere? If God is everything, how can there be matter which is not God? If God is all, how can man have freedom and choice? According to Luria and Hayim Vital, God was compelled to make room for the world by abandoning a region within Himself, a kind of mystical primordial space called tehiru, from which He withdrew in order to return to it in the act of creation. The first act of En-Sof is therefore not a step outside but a voluntary step inside, of movement, of self-limitation.

Side by side with this doctrine of tsimtsum, we find the doctrines of shevirat Hakelim and tikkun, the mending of a defect. The Kabbalists spoke of a divine light which flowed

from the essence of En-Sof into the primordial space of the
tsimtsum. This divine light was involved in the creation
process. This light or Godly power was housed in vessels,
kelippot. After the Adamic sin, the vessels were broken and the
light or Godly sparks, were scattered. The breaking of the
vessel is the decisive turning point in the cosmological process
of Luria. It is the cause of that inner deficiency which is
inherent in everything that exists and which persists as long as
the damage is not mended. The restoration of the ideal order,
the reuniting of the sparks with their divine source, is the
purpose of existence. Salvation means nothing but restitution
or re-integration of the original whole, or tikkun. The goal is
to restore the scattered lights of God to their proper place.

This brings us to the most revolutionary aspect of the
doctrine of tikkun, the point where the spiritual and the
political may converge. The process in which God conceives,
brings forth and develops Himself does not reach its final
conclusion in God. Certain critical parts of the process of
restitution are alloted to people. People must help release the
sparks; God can not do it alone. It is they who help perfect
God. The religious act of the individual prepares the way for
the final restitution of all exiled and scattered sparks. Man,
through his acts, has it in his power to hinder or accelerate
this process. Every act of man thus has cosmic repercussions.

It follows from this that for Luria the appearance of the
Messiah is nothing but the consummation of the continuous
process of tikkun. Redemption comes when everything is back in
its proper place and the blemish removed. It is here that we
have the point where the mystical, messianic and even
potentially political elements in Luria's doctrine are welded
together. Everything that man does reacts somewhere on this
process of tikkun. Every event and every domain of existence is
dependent on human activity. We are responsible and capable of
achieving our own salvation, be it messianic or secular. In a
sense, then, we are not only masters of our own destiny, we also
have a mission which goes far beyond that. The doctrine of
tikkun raised every Jew to the rank of a protagonist in the
great process of restitution-redemption.[28] The Kabbalah, a
suppressed and esoteric tradition, has, according to Gershom
Scholem, been the dialectical energy, the motor force, behind
the normative tradition. If he is correct, and I believe he is,
the conceptual infrastructure exists within the Jewish mystical
tradition for the conversation with the Marxist tradition that I

am suggesting is necessary. An additional plank for that bridge
of dialogue is provided by the insights of Martin Buber.

It is evident to those who are acquainted with Buber's
thought that he was influenced by this tradition and that the
parallels between Rosenzweig and him are remarkable and that
Buber carried this theology of inwardness and personal communion
to its completest formulation. Not only do they share a common
existentialist thinking, and a common opposition to idealism,
but they also emphasize alike a philosophy of dialogue: the
inter-relationship of God, world and man; the interworking of
creation, revelation and redemption; and the I-Thou interaction
between man and God. It was Buber's contention that man could
discover his own personality, his own "I" by saying "Thou" to
God, by entering into a kind of equal dialogue with God. By
addressing God as "Thou," by maintaining the tension of a
conversational attitude with God, man could approach the essence
of God; and by encountering that essence as an equal, man
exalted himself to the full extent of his divinity.[29]

The main formative influences on Buber during his early
years were the two great German mystics of the Middle Ages,
Meister Eckhart and Jakob Bohme. From them Buber derived his
concept of pantheism, the need for a deeper link with the
outside world, the unity of all living matter in God. There was
a God-given harmony in the world. Man had become alienated from
this harmony, but could return to it by listening to the voice
of inner experience, to intuition. Later on Buber discovered in
the ecstasy of the Hassidic sects of Eastern Europe, the genuine
mystical experience which led to unity with God and the world.
He deeply admired the "Hitlahavuth," the rapture with which the
Hasidim worshipped God, the complusion which drove the Hasidim
to search for God in the recesses of emotion rather than through
the process of reason. The Hasidim had learned a wondrous
truth; it was possible to enter into communion, indeed, into
dialogue with God. Buber introduced the forgotten Hassidic
legends to Western Europe, and provided a new Weltanschauung for
the young intellectuals seeking to return to Judaism.[30]

Never wavering from his philosophical beliefs, Buber
throughout his life stressed human action and human deed, human
participation in creation. In his book, The Prophetic Faith, he
writes of a divine-human "conjunction"; about the "partnership"
between man and the divine in the on-going creation of the
world.[31] In another work, the Eclipse of God, Buber talks
about human "participation in creation."[32]

Both Rosenzweig and Buber began their philosophizing from the idea of God as Creator. Theirs is not a God of commandment, not a God of the Midrash, but a God who is the ground of the ever-renewing basis of life. Human independence and human responsibility, according to Buber, are twin themes which complement this openness to the future. In the Eclipse of God, Buber states that God established man with "an independence which has since remained undiminished." He repeats similar concepts in The Prophetic Faith, where he asserts that God "works through the independence of man"; and, again, that "God acts through man." Freedom, independence and responsibility are all allied concepts. They are important concepts because they have added dignity and generative power to human existence. Furthermore, it is impossible to stress the importance of human deeds, human actions, unless one also assumes human freedom and responsibility.

In the spirit of the prophets, Buber stresses the notion of historicity. For Buber, the historical is not reduced to a succession of concentration camps. Through human decisions taking place in time, man can "cooperate in the redemption of the world" (Israel and the World).[33] Buber likes to talk about human "beginnings," and when he does so he touches again upon the central concept of on-going creation. But it is impossible to talk of continuous creation, without assuming the dignity, as well as the redemptive power, of the historical. One of Buber's basic themes is the saving mission of history as it proceeds and emanates from the source of human deed and decision.

The theology of Rosenzweig and Buber, as well as the insights of the Kabbalah, can thus serve as a bridge between Judaism and Marxist thought. The paths of 20th century Jewish theology and 20th century Marxist theory cross and meet at several conceptions. The Marxist notions of anthropological immanence, of praxis, of critical activity are consonant with the Rosenzweig-Buber ideas of human participation in creation, in the redemptive quality of human actions. In addition, the Marxist commitment to historicity, to future, to societal transformation, corresponds to the Rosenzweig-Buber modern Messianic faith in history. Stressing the goodness of God in creation, Rosenzweig-Buber relate to the historical as continuous becoming-into-being, as renewal, as beginning, and such ideas mirror the Marxist dedication to hope, to the transcending power of negation. Lastly, the conceptions of objectificaton, of externalization and of value in Being, which

are so central to Marxist ethics, overlap and cohere to the
Rosenzweig-Buber idea of human decision, of man who must act
because human deed is a necessary conjuntion with Divine. For
Buber and Rosenzweig, people are required to act, because only
through their action is creation reaffirmed and supported in its
continuity; in this co-sponsorship in creation, man finds
encounter with the divinity.

A Jewish-Marxist conversation would bring needed renewal to
Jewish thought. It would also reveal how the post-Holocaust
Jewish fear and retreat from history could be transcended.
Through this encounter, Jewish thought would be helped to return
to its classical and mystical dimension, to a Messianic
expectation of the future. Living in history, instead of
history being seen as an endless grave, would again become a
redemptive exercise.

Furthermore, Jewish thought would again be redevoted to the
prophetic quest for social justice. A Judaism which confined
itself to interpretive activity, to study and analysis alone,
would either be idealist in character or, by laying all the
emphasis on the transformation of consciousness, would leave
untouched that dualism of life and thought that Marx criticized
in Feuerbach. History demands not merely to be interpreted, but
to be changed. And it is not only our consciousness that needs
to be changed, but the circumstances in which that consciousness
finds expression. Judaism is not redemptive if it merely
interprets. It is our circumstances and not simply our states
of mind, that cry out for redemptive transformation. Only a
form of Jewish life and activity which contributed, in fact, to
the liberating transformation of the material circumstances of
human existence could be said to be materialist in the Marxist
sense.

There is no doubt that Judaism is, in principle, compatible
with commitment to revolutionary struggle. For a number of
reasons, however, Jewish participation in that struggle should
be ambiguous. In the first place, the Jewish community should
always include elements which insist on standing aside from the
struggle to bear witness to the partial and provisional nature
of the historically realizable transformation of social
reality. There must always be a divine input as well. In the
second place, in the course of the revolution, Jewish
participation should include the reminder that the use of force
is always morally ambiguous and infected by corruption and evil
(killing is not, and can never be, an act of compassion and

love), and that not all means are appropriate in pursuit of even the most admirable ends.

If the foregoing argument is correct, there still do exist strong threads of continuity with the Jewish past. As much as ever, Jews should insist with the confidence of their tradition, that the exercise of power be tempered by a moral and by a politically transforming vision. Judaism, like Marxism, looks forward to the total redemption of humanity. Both Judaism and Marxism refuse to accept the insurmountability of human transcendence. Karl Marx, despite repeated attacks upon the Jewish spirit, may have been more responsive to his Jewish antecedents than he realized. He believed as a matter of faith that the complicated world of social and economic phenomena could be subsumed under general scientific laws. He interpreted history not as some aimless and haphazard succession of events, but as embodying a pattern that should be understood dialectically and teleologically, as progress from lower to higher levels of social organization leading ultimately to liberation. Finally, he predicated his activity in a prophetic mode on the certainty that eventually a new age would be ushered in in which political domination would cease and each person would experience full creative potential and exercise full authority over himself. Marxism thus is more than a mere strategy of political action, more than a program of economic and social reconstruction, more even than a comprehensive theory of history and society. As traditional Judaism declines in impact, many Jews may divert their Messianic urges into Marxism as a kind of surrogate religion. The secular Jew with a misty background of Talmudic dialectic and infused with a tradition of Judaic social justice might be seen as intellectually predisposed to Marxism to a degree that s/he rarely appreciates. Marxist thought may become for them an ethic, a theology; it is cerebral, almost Talmudic in its logic; a vast, all-embracing doctrine of man and the universe; a passionate faith endowing life with meaning; an optimistic view of man and the future that can jell very well with the prophetic and mystical impulse in Judaism. As I have attempted to argue, this is a political vision not entirely foreign to the Jewish experience.

CHURCH-SECT THEORY, RELIGIOUS AUTHORITY, AND
MODERN JEWISH ORTHODOXY:
A CASE STUDY

David Ellenson
Hebrew Union College-Jewish Institute of Religion

Peter Berger has observed that a major result of the process
of secularization in the modern world is that "sectors of
society and culture are removed from the domination of religious
symbols and institutions."[1] Institutions and persons once
controlled by religion have been removed from such tutelage.
This process of secularization has not only had effects upon the
role religion plays in society, but upon traditional religions
themselves. As Berger says, "The fundamental problem of
[traditional] religious institutions is how to keep going in a
milieu that no longer takes for granted their definitions of
reality."[2] In brief, the advent of modernity and the rise of
secularization have caused the plausibility structure which
supported the institutions and worldviews of medieval Western
religious traditions to crumble or, at the very least, to be
severely challenged.

Judaism, for example, in its medieval Central European
manifestation, was established upon the basis of a corporate
political structure which granted the Jewish community a
position of semi-autonomous political power and upon an
intellectual foundation which both regarded Jewish law as
divinely revealed and saw the rabbis as the legitimate
expositors of that law. The intellectual underpinning of this
system, however, began to flounder in the seventeenth century
under the attacks of Spinoza, and by the nineteenth century
large numbers of Jews in Germany and Western Europe no longer
accepted the religious discipline upon which medieval rabbinic
Judaism had rested. In addition, the abrogation of rabbinic
civil authority in most of the German states by 1811 meant finis
for the political structure which had supported medieval
rabbinic traditionalism in that region. Consequently, Judaism
in nineteenth century Germany faced a crisis of unprecedented
proportions. The German Jewish leadership of this period,
caught in this maelstrom of change, had to take cognizance of
these shifts in their efforts to exercise leadership in the
German Jewish community of the 1800s.

The problem was particularly acute for the Orthodox Jews of
this time and place. Unlike their Liberal colleagues, who

accepted the notion of historical development in Judaism, the Orthodox were wedded to the traditional theological notion that God's revelation to the Jewish people, eternal and immutable, had been delivered through Moses at Sinai. Thus, contemporary intellectual trends which caused large masses of Jews in nineteenth century Germany to abandon both the beliefs and practices of traditional rabbinic Judaism were resisted by the Orthodox. On the other hand, these German Orthodox Jews, products of a Western cultural milieu, affirmed the political developments of the contemporary era. In addition to their acceptance of the political benefits Emancipation had to confer on them, these Orthodox Jews also accepted the value and worth of modern Western culture; they mastered German and adopted many of the manners of nineteenth century German society. In affirming both modernity and aspects of Jewish tradition and identity, these Jews established a pattern which modern Orthodox Jews in Western lands have continued to follow to this day. Their efforts extend beyond their day into our own.

Here, in an attempt to understand the nature of this affirmation, I propose to employ a framework of church-sect typology and apply it to an analysis of Rabbi Esriel Hildesheimer's approach to the problem of religious authority as it presented itself to the Orthodox Jewish community of nineteenth century Germany. Indeed, in employing this typology, I am consiously following the suggestion offered by Arnold Eisen, who, in an essay entitled "The uses of Social Theory in the Study of Modern Judaism," has written that "using the lens . . . provided by social theory, . . . we discover how much more . . . the new lens enables us to see, and we assess the importance of what we come to see . . . within the materials of modern Judaism as a whole."[3] For, by utilizing aspects of church-sect theory in this case study, aspects of the response Judaism has made to modernity will be clarified and the nature of the Jewish reaction to the demands of the modern situation illuminated.

Hildesheimer (1820-1899), who served in both Eisenstadt, Hungary, and Berlin during his rabbinical career, was most famous for his establishment of the Orthodox Berlin Rabbinical Seminary in 1873. Scion of a traditional rabbinic family, Hildesheimer was exposed as a youth to the culture and worldview of traditional rabbinic civilization, but was also immersed in the culture of the contemporary Western world and in 1846 became one of the first Orthodox rabbis in Germany to receive a secular doctorate. As a result, Hildesheimer reflected values and outlooks common to both worlds.[4] It is precisely because Hildesheimer represented this position that he provides a paradigmatic example of how Judaism in general and Modern Orthodoxy in particular responded to the tensions inherent in this new era. Furthermore, as German rabbis of the nineteenth century could no longer exercise imperative authority, the issue of religious authority serves as a useful focus for an investigation of how Judaism both evolved and remained constant in regard to social change. For these rabbis had to devise new stratagems to achieve influential religous authority in the German-Jewish context.[5]

This study begins with a consideration of church-sect typology in the sociology of religion. It then moves on, in light of this theory, to a consideration of Hildesheimer's activities in regard to the issue of religious authority. A summary of Hildesheimer's initial efforts in this area in his home province of Saxony from 1847 to 1849 will be followed by an analysis of his activities in Eisenstadt from 1851 to 1869. Finally, the mature Hildesheimer's approach to the question of religious authority in Berlin from 1869 to the end of his life will be discussed. In this way the direction taken by Modern Orthodox Judaism in the contemporary world will be illuminated and the adequacy of church-sect theory to clarify something of the nature of modern Judaism will be revealed.

II

Ernst Troeltsch developed a well-known typology of religious groups based upon a distinction between "church" and "sect." Troeltsch defined the "church" as universalistic in nature. The church was seen as non-dogmatic and ideologically flexible. Anxious to include as many persons as possible under its umbrella, the church aims "to extend its ministry to everyone. As a result, it must be willing 'to compromise with the wide range of behaviors that may be found in a society.'"[6] It is this remarkably flexible, non-dogmatic character which aids the church in attracting large numbers of adherents. A second characteristic which the church generally evidences also contributes to its potential success as a religious organization able to attract large numbers. For, as Benton Johnson has written, the major characteristic defining the church is that a "church is a religious group that accepts the social environment in which it exists,"[7] or, as Stephen Steinberg has amended it,

is "in low tension with the social environment."[8] This
position allows the church to accommodate itself to the larger
social environment and permits the religion to organize its
institutions and worldview in order to be more "relevant" and
hence more "influential" in the contemporary world. Both major
features of the church -- its non-dogmatic nature and its
acceptance of the social environment -- contribute to its
success as a religious grouping.

In contrast to the church, the "sect" is highly ideological
and dogmatic in nature. Hence, sects are generally rather
small, cohesive religious units. As Charles Liebman phrases it:

> The sect is a smaller group arising from the inability of
> the church to meet some members' needs by virtue of its very
> flexibility and adaptability. The sect repudiates "the
> compromises of the church, preferring isolation to
> compromise."[9]

Moreover, the sect, in contradistinction to the church, is, in
Johnson's words, "a religious group that rejects the social
environment in which it exists,"[10] or, as Steinberg puts it,
"is in high tension with the social environment."[11] The
appeal of the sect to large numbers of persons is thus
constricted by its resistance to the contemporary cultural
world. Yet, as Liebman has pointed out, these very qualities
contribute to the sect's success in attracting certain persons
to its fold.

It is vital to note that church-sect theory has been the
object of considerable criticsm and revision by sociologists of
religion during the last fifty years. H. Richard Neibuhr,[12]
Liston Pope,[13] and others have refined the approach of
church-sect theory to the nature of religious organizations by
adding a third category to the ideal types of church and sect --
the denomination. As sects accommodate the patterns of the
larger society, they invariably evolve sequentially into
denominations. While they manage to maintain a certain
distinctiveness, the process of routinization causes them to
achieve a state of low tension with the social environment.
Still other students of church-sect theory have claimed that not
all sects follow this pattern of development. J. Milton
Yinger[14] and Bryan Wilson,[15] for example, speak of a
typology of sects which manage to maintain themselves in
opposition to, or non-acceptance of, the values and worldview of
secular society over a considerable period of time. Rodney
Stark and William Brainbridge, having noted that "church-sect
conceptualization is too limited to serve fully the needs of a

theory of religious movements,"[16] add another ideal type -- the cult -- to this typology.[17] In short, advocates of church-sect theory and its application to the study of religious organizations have noted that the typology needs constant refinement to be employed fruitfully as a heuristic device in the analysis of religious groupings.[18]

In the case of contemporary Jewish religious groups, one such refinement has been offered by Charles Liebman.[19] While Liebman adopts a two-dimensional model of church-sect typology -- acceptance/rejection of the social environment and flexibility versus dogmatism in the area of ideology -- as providing the definitional base against which he identifies and measure modern Jewish religious groupings, he adds that church-sect theory in this classical form is not fully applicable to the case of contemporary Judaism. This is because the typology, in Leibman's words, "assumes a closed society in which the religious order is confronted only by the secular order and the individual needs of its members." However, as a result of the religious pluralism created in the Jewish world by the advent of modernity, religious groups within Judaism must confront not only the problem of dealing with the larger secular society and the religious needs of the individual within that secular societal setting. They must also adopt a policy vis-a-vis other religious groups in Jewish society and confront the religious needs of the Jewish individual within that Jewish setting as well. Moreover, this problem, while present for all groups in Jewish society, is particularly severe for the Orthodox, Liebman asserts, for the doctrines of Orthodoxy require Orthodoxy to see itself as the sole legitimate bearer of Jewish tradition in the modern world. Jewish religious groups, in contradistinction to Christian ones, face a "double bind" in the modern world, for Jewish religious groups must articulate one position in regard to the larger society and another vis-a-vis other denominations within Judaism. The student of church-sect typology who would apply this framework to the study of religious groups in modern Judaism must keep Liebman's insight in mind when studying contemporary Jewish religious denominations. Otherwise, the utility of the theory may be reduced.[20]

An illustration of this can be found in the work of Stephen Steinberg on the development of Reform Judaism during the last two centuries in Western Europe and the United States. Reform Judaism, according to Steinberg, constitutes an "anomaly" among

church movements because Reform originally enunciated a
universalistic system of theology which caused it to modify
"institutional norms and values that were discrepant with those
of the larger [secular] society."[21] This spirit of
accommodation to the demands of the secular world precluded
Reform being labelled a sect while its origins as a movement in
little or no tension with the social environment indicated that
Reform did not follow the sequential pattern socioligists
identified as typical of a denomination. Yet, through its
enunciation in 1885 of the Pittsburgh Platform, which
dogmatically illustrated "the [Reform] Movement's objective of
greater conformity to the norms and values of Western society"
and its simultaneous rejection of traditional rabbinic notions
of revelation and ritual practice, Reform evidenced, in
Steinberg's words, characteristics of "a sectarian movement"
vis-a-vis the traditionalists in the Jewish community.[22] As a
result, Steinberg concluded that Reform was a churchlike
religious movement and that traditional theories about such
religious movements and the directions in which they evolve had
to be revised to account for the case of Reform Judaism.

However, Steinberg's position -- that an entire theory needs
to be amended to account for the case of Reform Judaism -- is,
it seems to me, less helpful in clarifying the phenomenon of
Reform Judaism in the modern world than is Liebman's insight.
Indeed, Liebman's insight concerning the double bind which
religious groups in modern Judaism confront in adapting
themselves to both secular and Jewish society would encourage
the student of modern Judaism who utilizes church-sect typology
as a heuristic device for the illumination of Judaism in the
modern world to recongnize the potential dual nature of a
particular Jewish religious group's response to the challenge
presented it by the modern situation. Moreover, as Liebman
assets, "to the extent that [a] . . . denomination stresses the
solution to one order of problems it raises questions for the
other."[23] Thus, in analyzing the case of Reform Judaism
through the lens of church-sect theory as provided by Liebman,
the observer need not hasten to label the movement either a
"church" or "sect." Instead, one can note that Reform was
churchlike in its attitude toward secular society and, informed
by that attitude, was sectarian in regard to traditional Jewish
society. Leibman's approach has the advantage of viewing the
response of Judaism to the conditions posed by modernity in all
its complexity.

It is in the light of Liebman's insight that I want to
examine Hildesheimer's approach to the problem of religious
authority, for the application of this insight will help to
explain the nature of Modern Jewish Orthodoxy and its responses
to the modern world. The Modern Orthodox, as exemplified by
this material, were in a state of low tension with secular
society insofar as they affirmed the value and worth of modern
Western culture. Simultaneously, however, this posture led them
to assume a position of separation from the traditionalist
Orthodox, who eschewed this affirmation. Furthermore, their
commitment to traditional rabbinic notions of revelation and
practice moved the Modern Orthodox to adopt increasingly
sectarian stance vis-a-vis other religious groups in the Jewish
community which did not share this commitment. My analysis will
reveal this pattern, will clarify the nature of Modern Jewish
Orthodoxy, and will also illustrate the utility of church-sect
theory, in this modified form, for a clarification of the Jewish
response to the modern world.

II

Hildesheimer, upon the completion of his doctoral studies at
the University of Halle in 1846, returned to his hometown of
Halberstadt to assume the post of secretary to the Jewish
community. It was the first time that the twenty-six year old
Orthodox rabbi had assumed a puiblic role in Jewish communal
affairs. The traditional nature of the community was just
beginning to change and Reform Judaism, through the work of
Ludwig Philippson, was beginning to make its influence felt. On
March 3, 1847, a law was passed permitting Jews to come before
the secular authorities for permission to secede "from the
community to which they are attached."[24] Consequently, eight
Jewish citizens applied to the secular authorities of
Halberstadt for permission to leave the Orthodox-controlled
organized Jewish community. This action precipitated a crisis
for the Orthodox leadership of the Halberstadt community --
Hildesheimer and Rabbi Mattathias Levian -- and both men
responded to the Reformers. A scrutiny of Hildesheimer's
activities in this crisis will underscore the dual "church-sect"
nature of his brand of Orthodoxy, for while he affirmed the
manners, political view, and culture of contemporary Germany
through his activities, he simultaneously, on account of his
religious ideology, assumed a stance which would ultimately lead
him into a sectarian position vis-a-vis the Reformers, whom he
regarded as deviants from authentic Judaism.

Hildesheimer was not inclined to content himself with simply attacking the Reformers. He directly addressed the governing board of the Halberstadt municipality which had the final say in this affair, and the acculturated Jews in the community who had to be persuaded that continued Orthodox domination in communal affairs was desirable. Undoubtedly prompted by this event, Hildesheimer, in 1849, wrote a German pamphlet (<u>Administration of the Halberstadt Jewish Community</u>) to present the case before these two groups for continued Orthodox domination in communal affairs. In this work, Hildesheimer traced the administration of the Halberstadt Jewish community historically and argued that the Orthodox had competently managed the affairs of the community both before and after the turn of the century.[25] By writing this piece in German in accordance with the academic standards of the day, Hildesheimer was not only displaying a prudential ability to exercise influential religious authority in an era when imperative authority had been wrested from the rabbinate, but was also affirming both the worth of as well as his mastery of secular culture. Such an interpretation is strengthened by analysis of a Hebrew responsum he wrote on the subject.

Hildesheimer's responsum, written in respectful terms to his senior colleage Levian, said that to engage in invective against these men was unwise. While he was equally critical of their views, as a modern who affirmed the manners of nineteenth century Germany, he was careful to avoid a pre-modern style of incivility against these Reformers. Thus, Hildesheimer, in testimony he delivered before the Halberstadt municipality against the Reformers, indicated that he had no wish to engage in invective and charge them with "apostasy." This obviously could have been interpreted as an attamept to infrige upon their right of freedom of conscience. Consequently, Hildesheimer simply claimed that these Reformers wished to avoid their civic duty in order "to escape paying communal taxes." Hildesheimer's sensitivities to the demands of contemporary manners and values is apparent here. In addition, Hildesheimer voiced a positive opinion of the political position Jews enjoyed in mid-nineteenth century Germany. For, he stated, "in this generation, with the mercy of the Most High, . . . there is no need for this alienation from our Father in Heaven in order to achieve this goal [of civil equality]."[26] Hildesheimer did not perceive Germany as a land of "bitter Exile" and he claimed that the Jews of Halberstadt lived under no threat of "subjugation or

persecution." Hildesheimer's affirmative attitude towards
political developments in nineteenth century Germany, combined
with his acceptance of nineteenth century German cultural forms
and manners, reveals that his Orthodoxy was not sectarian in
respect to the larger German society. Indeed, his was a
"churchlike" German Jewish Orthodoxy in respect to the secular
environment.

All this, however, should not obsure the fact that he was an
intractable opponent of Reform. In the body of the Hebrew
responsum he wrote, Hildesheimer did charge the Reformers with
being sectarians, and labelled them as those "who separate
themselves from the ways of the community." Consequently,
Hildesheimer ruled that these men could not be buried in a
Jewish cemetery, could not be included in a Jewish prayer
quorum, could not be called to a public reading of the Torah,
and could not recite the mourner's prayer on behalf of a
deceased relative unless there was no one else to do so. He did
not rule on whether these persons could be married in a Jewish
weding ceremony. The seeds of what ultimately would come to be
a sectarian position in regard to other religious groups in
Judaism are clearly present here in the young Hildesheimer's
commitment to traditional Jewish religious dogma. Another event
in 1847 underscores this view of Hildesheimer's "churchlike"
posture in regard to secular society and his "sectarian" stance
vis-a-vis other religious groups in Judaism.

On September 15, 1847, the governing board of the Magdeburg
Jewish community, at the instigation of Ludwig Philippson,
issued an invitation to representatives of all the Jewish
communities in Saxony to come to Magdeburg for a provincial
assembly. Hildesheimer, along with his brother-in-law Joseph
Hirsch, represented Halberstadt at the mid-October conference.
At the conference, Philippson made several requests, two of
which are of particular significance for our purposes. The
first was a proposal that the delegates pass a resolution
recommending the adoption of an "alteration and adjustment of
the divine service" to be used in the synagogues of Saxony.[27]
In making such a suggestion, Philippson was, in effect, asking
the assembly to recognize reform as a legitimate element in
Judaism.

Philippson's second request was that the assembly pass a
resolution formally separating the "synagogue community" in each
town from the "total community." The Reformers, in the 1840s,
were still the minority in most of the Jewish communities.

Consequently, the Orthodox, who dominated most communities, were able to place a check upon their demands for reform. By advocating such a resolution, Philippson was proposing the establishment of an autonomous foundation for the growth of Reform in each of these communities apart from the inhibiting checks proposed by an Orthodox majority. Moreover, the implication to be drawn from this was that Philippson was simply asking the convention to affirm the principle of freedom of religious conscience. For, in making this proposal, Philippson was not asking the convention to ratify reform as a legitimate element in Judaism as he did with his first proposal. Rather, he simply asked that the basic right of freedom of religious conscience be given to the Reformers to work out their own approach to the Jewish religion in their own way.

Here the dilemma confronting Hildesheimer -- a dilemma that stemmed from the double nature of the response modernity requires of Judaism -- is most apparent. As a modern who took a "churchlike" approach to the values and worth of Western culture, Hildesheimer could not allow himself to appear opposed to contemporary notions of religious freedom. On the other hand, as an Orthodox Jew committed to certain uncompromisable notions of divine revelation, he could not support Philippson's proposals without paving the way for the growth of Reform. Moreover, as we shall see, Hildesheimer still felt it possible, in 1847, for the Orthodox to remain the dominant force in the Jewish community. He was not yet prepared to enunciate a fully sectarian position in regard to other elements in the Jewish religious community.

Hildesheimer responded, then, by leaving the convention and writing a series of German articles in Der Orient, a Leipzing-based periodical, explaining the traditionalists' stance.[28] Hildesheimer claimed that he and the other delegates had been brought to Magdeburg under false pretenses. In addition, he claimed that the delegates were not truly representative of their communities and, in voting for these resolutions, had been guilty of attempting to force their views on the Jews of the province. Here Hildesheimer, as a man of nineteenth century German culture appealing his case before an acculturated Jewish community, clearly argued on nineteenth century grounds. By charging the Reformers with deceit in calling the convention and by claiming that the assembly had violated the rules of fundamental democracy, Hildesheimer was stating that the Reformers, not the Orthodox, were guilty of violating the canons of nineteenth century parliamentarianism. His churchlike affirmation of the larger society and its values is here apparent.

Hildesheimer went on, however, to argue that even a representative assembly would not have had the authority to act on these proposals since the representatives, as laypersons who were Jewishly ignorant, had no authority to act on the proposals. In other words, the issue was really not one of democracy. It was one of proper religious authority. Hildesheimer's sectarian affirmation of rabbinic religious dogma placed him in an intellectual bind, for his adoption of a churchlike posture in regard to the values of secular society, combined with affirmation of a sectarian, dogmatic posture in regard to creed, testifies that the dual response which a Jewish religious group may make to both secular and Jewish societies may sometimes be in conflict. Thus, while these episodes in the life of the young Hildesheimer indicate that his view of modern society was essentially positive, and that he still hoped to maintain Orthodox domination over the rest of the community, his commitment to traditional rabbinic dogma meant, as we shall see, that his policy of sectarianism vis-a-vis the rest of the Jewish religious community was inevitably going to crystallize itself fully in the decades ahead.

III

Well versed in rabbinics, armed with a secular doctorate, and famed as a fighter against Reform, Hildesheimer, by 1851, was esteemed by many in the Orthodox Jewish world as a religious leader capable of meeting the challenges of modernity. Consequently, in 1851, the very important Hungarian community of Eisenstadt elected Hildesheimer as rabbi.[29] Eisenstadt, though it "remained in the Orthodox camp,"[30] had, because of its proximity to Vienna, been exposed to Western cultural influences and sheltered a number of Orthodox Jews who affirmed and valued Western culture while simultaneously clinging to the traditional doctrine of divine legitimation for the Halakha (Jewish law). Hildesheimer was instructed to devote his major efforts to education[31] and, immediately on his arrival in Eisenstadt, established the first yeshiva in the Western world to include secular subjects in its curriculum.[32] Hildesheimer decided to employ German, rather than Yiddish, as the language of instruction in his yeshiva -- which set the yeshiva apart in the Hungary of his day. The reason for this was his feeling that Orthodoxy could not be spread among the acculturated segments of Central European Jewry if the Orthodox religious leadership of the community was not suitably equipped, as Hildesheimer would phrase it, "to fight the war on behalf of Torah and her commandments."[33] Hildesheimer's concern was not merely prudential, however. His commitment to the worth of Western culture and society was substantive as well. He would not surrender that commitment despite the fact that such churchlike affirmation and acceptance of secular culture and manners alienated him from the sectarian Orthodox who resided in Hungary.[34]

These sectarian Orthodox Jews held, as one rabbi put it, that a Jew who spoke a non-Jewish language such as German or Hungarian, was to be considered a "gentile"; they distrusted Hildesheimer from the beginning of his stay in Hungary. Hildesheimer's adopton of Western modes of dress, his decision to utilize the vernacular in his yeshiva and his introduction of secular subjects into the curriculum of the yeshiva all made Hildesheimer a dangerous character in their eyes. One Hasidic rebbe, Akiba Yoseph Schlesinger, pronounced a ban of excommunication upon Hildesheimer and charged that only sinners who caused others to sin emerged from the Eisenstadt yeshiva.[35] Similarly, Hillel Lichtenstein, Schlesinger's father-in-law, branded Hildesheimer "a man of deceit, a liar, . . . wrapped, so to speak, in a garb of righteousness which outwardly justifies his deed, like a pig that stretches forth its hoofs."[36] These statements, extreme though they are, should not be seen simply as the zealous pronouncements of two fanatics. Rather, it should be evident that what separated these men and their version of Orthodoxy from Hildesheimer and his version was a vast difference in approach to modern culture. The sectarian Orthodox determinedly resisted the blandishments of modernity and spurned the value of secular society. Hildesheimer, with his positive attitude toward Western culture, was anathema in their eyes in spite of their shared attitudes regarding the divine revelation of Torah. Their consistent hostility to both secular society and other religious groupings within Judaism alienated them from Hildesheimer, who would not abandon his attachment to Western culture.

Hildesheimer, throughout his years in Hungary, supported the notion of a modern Orthodox rabbinical seminary. The rest of the Hungarian Orthodox rabbinate, fearful of the establishment of a rabbinical school in which secular subjects would be taught and contemporary methods of study employed, vehemently opposed the creation of such a school and preferred the retention of rabbinical academies which would eschew secular learning.[37] Even Hildesheimer's closest friend in Hungary, Rabbi Judah Assad, who sympathized with Hildesheimer's attitude to secular culture, urged him not to disavow publicly the Orthodox opposition to the creation of a modern rabbinical seminary. Nevertheless, Hildesheimer set aside his friend's counsel and chose instead to write a letter publicly indicating his support for such an institution. This letter, which brought the wrath of the sectarian Orthodox down upon Hildesheimer's head, is an indication that his churchlike affirmation of Western culture was not simply pragmatic.[38]

The rift between Hildesheimer and the sectarian Orthodox fully emerged in 1866. The Orthodox rabbinate of Hungary, concerned over the advances being made by the Reformers, assembled at Mihalowitz to issue guidelines which would instruct communities as to the reforms they should resist.[39] The conference passed nine resolutions in which it called, among other things, for a ban against preaching in a non-Jewish language. The rabbis also warned Jews not to enter a synagogue with a tower, which they felt imitated the architectural style of a church, and rabbis and cantors were not allowed to don clerical robes, lest they appear like officiants of other religions. These rabbis issued a ban against entering a synagogue which featured a choir, even if the choir was all-male, and forbade weddings to take place inside a synagogue. Instead, the rabbis insisted that the Hungarian Jewish custom of holding weddings outdoors had to be maintained. Finally, they prohibited change in any custom or synagogue practice handed down from previous generations. Obviously, the sectarian Orthodox were not only attempting to combat Reform, but were also intent on rejecting aesthetic and other changes in Jewish prayer and synagogue life which would be in keeping with the cultural mores and patterns of nineteenth century society. The Hungarians raised such issues to the level of religious questions precisely because their sectarian posture and subsequent rejection of the nineteenth century cultural world caused them to view these items not as matters of taste, but as matters of religious import. Indeed, their strong resistance to secular society bespoke an obscurantist antagonism not only to the larger society and groups such as the Reformers

in Jewish society, but to a modern Orthodox proponent like
Hildesheimer as well.

Hildesheimer, of course, opposed these Hungarian rabbis and
their attitude to questions which he saw primarily as
inconsequential for matters of religious faith. His Western
aesthetic sensibilities allowed Hildesheimer to be comfortable
with modernist reforms which were not, in his opinion, at odds
with Jewish law. Indeed, he himself favored many of these
reforms on prudential grounds as necessary stratagems for the
preservation of Orthodoxy in the modern era. Through their
rejection of secular culture, it seemed to Hildesheimer, the
sectarian Orthodox were guilty of "burying their head in the
sand" and refusing to acknowledge contemporary realities.[40]
Their stance would only serve to weaken the position of the
Orthodox among acculturated segments of the Hungarian Jewish
community.[41] As Hildesheimer observed, it was essential for
the Orthodox to discover "a way which finds assent and favor in
the eyes of the majority of the people."[42]

Hildesheimer's position remained a lonely one in the
Orthodox camp, and throughout the 1860's he found himself
increasingly isolated from his Orthodox colleagues. At the
Hungarian Jewish Congress of 1869, all the proposals he offered
and evey position he favored were roundly denounced by the
sectarian Orthodox.[43] In a letter to Judah Assad,
Hildesheimer confessed that his isolation in the Orthodox camp
wounded him deeply and personally.[44]

During these same years Hildesheimer's modernism did not
interfere with his firm commitment to traditional Jewish notions
of revelation. In instances where Jewish law and the values of
modern society clashed, he had no doubt that preference had to
be given to Jewish law.[45] Similarly, when discussing why
Jewish law disqualified certain categories of people (e.g.,
women) from offering testimony at some Jewish legal proceedings,
Hildesheimer asserted that such disabilities were beyond human
understanding; they conformed to God's will.[46] While
Hildesheimer recognized that Jewish law could permit a variety
of interpretations, no compromise could be made with the
principle that the "Torah had been revealed from the mouth of
the Almighty."[47]

Such a commitment to traditional rabbinic theology only
roused the ire of the Reformers, who were particularly anxious
to discredit Hildesheimer in the eyes of the acculturated
segments of Hungarian Jewry. The Reformers, anxious for a full

hegemony among these elements in the community, felt that a serious religious rigidity lay hidden behind Hildesheimer's modernism -- his intellectual attainments, his inclusion of secular subjects in his yeshiva's curriculum, his constant attention to secular modes of argumentation, his sensitivity to nineteenth century aesthetic standards and mores. Again and again Leopold Loew, the leading non-Orthodox rabbi in Hungary, attacked Hildesheimer and his yeshiva in an attempt to discredit Hildesheimer's scholarship and the level of study in his yeshiva.[48] In addition, the Reformers wanted to depict him as a rigid fundamentalist who rejected contemporary standards of biblical scholarship.[49] No less than the sectarian Orthodox, the Reformers were troubled by a man like Hildesheimer whose affirmation of modern culture had led him into a "churchlike" attitude to secular society and whose commitment to traditional Jewish dogma had caused him to adopt a sectarian stance regarding non-Orthodox religionists.

Hildesheimer's experience in Hungary altered his views on the question of religious authority. Prior to his years there, Hildesheimer still felt it possible for the Orthodox to attain hegemony over the rest of the Jewish religious community. By the 1860's he understood clearly that any dream of a united Jewish religious community was a chimera. The strength of Reform and of secularism was too great to be eradicated. Consequently, he came to favor a division of the religious community along Reform-Orthodox lines.[50] The position of the sectarian Orthodox, with their absolute rejection of modern culture, meant, of course, that he could have no influence among them. Thus, Hildesheimer was prepared to speak only to those among the acculturated in the community who would affirm the principles of a Modern Jewish Orthodoxy -- an Orthodoxy committed to the worth of secular culture while simultaneously clinging to the belief in "Torah from Heaven."

In summary, it was Hildesheimer's churchlike affirmation of modern culture which allowed him to address himself to acculturated members of the Jewish community, but he realized that this stance inevitably alienated him from the sectarian Orthodox. Similarly, his religious dogmatism prevented him from exercising influential religious authority among the Reformers. Nevertheless, Hildesheimer would not spend his energies on regret; he would acknowledge reality and resign himself to the circumstance that any attempt on his part to speak to non-Orthodox Jewish bodies or persons on religious questions was

futile. His formulation of Modrn Jewish Orthodoxy, in
contradistinction to sectarian Orthodoxy and Liberal Judaism
alike, is reflected in Liebman's observation about the "double
bind" which the modern Jewish religious leader confronts
vis-a-vis secular society on the one hand and Jewish religious
groups on the other. It reveals the distinctiveness of the
Hildesheimer position and the fact that the dual "church-sect"
nature of Modern Orthodoxy was already emergent in
Hildesheimer's thought by 1869 -- the year Hildesheimer decided
to accept an invitation to become rabbi of the separatist
Orthodox congregations Adass Jisroel in Berlin. At Berlin in
1869 the mature Hildesheimer's approach to the problem of
religious authority and the dual "church-sect" nature of Modern
Jewish Orthodoxy become fully apparent.

IV

Elchanan Rothstein, one of two remaining Orthodox rabbis in
Berlin died in 1869, and 800 traditional members of the Berlin
Jewish community petitioned the communal board to appoint a
rabbi who combined a university education, a thorough knowledge
of Talmud, and a commitment to Jewish tradition. The petition
had no impact on the board and Abraham Geiger, the leading
Reformer in contemporary Germany, was selected as the new
rabbi. Indeed, the chairman of the communal board declared
Orthodoxy "legally extinct among us."[51] At this point the
Orthodox decided to organize themselves and search for a new
rabbi to be paid out of private rather than communal funds. In
June, 1869, several prominent families established Congregation
Adass Jisroel.[52]

Hildesheimer had already confessed, ". . . Here [in Hungary]
I find little understanding of my principles."[53] He was ready
by 1869 to come to Berlin. The Berlin opportunity meant that
Hildesheimer would be settling in a thriving metropolis with a
large Jewish population receptive to his notions of "a cultured
Orthodoxy." As leader of an acculturated separatist Orthodox
community, Hildesheimer would be unhampered either by sectarian
Orthodoxy or Reform and could develop his plans for achieving
Orthodox religious authority. He finally had the forum he had
desired so long to actualize his program for religious authority.

For "cultured Orthodoxy" to flourish -- that is, an
Orthodoxy which joined "a faithful adherence to traditional
teachings with an effective effort to keep in touch with the
spirit of progress"[54] -- a sympathetic, receptive Orthodox

leadership had to be trained. The necessity for the creation of a modern Orthodox rabbinical seminary was more pressing than ever, and in 1873 the doors of a modern Orthodox rabbinical seminary reflecting Hildesheimer's ideals opened in Berlin with Hildesheimer at the head. The goal of the seminary was, in Hildesheimer's words, "to combat the destructive ambitions of the Reformers and to answer the demands of the time."[55] The simultaneous sectarian and churchlike nature of Modern Orthodoxy is herein revealed, for both his attack on Reform and his affirmation of modern culture are evident in this statement. The students at his seminary, he was sure, would be "imbued with Torah and fear of God," and, at the same time, would "be armed with science."[56] Thus, Hildesheimer had created his primary means for exerting influence and authority on the acculturated Jews of Germany who still clung to an observance of Jewish law and tradition. Yet, he had no illusions that the formation of the seminary would permit his religious authority to be exercised among all segments of the community. Indeed, three major episodes indicate that Hildesheimer was content to accept this limitation on his religious authority. He actually felt -- in light of the futility which would defeat any effort to impose Orthodox authority on the community as a whole -- that a self-imposed sectarian stance on reaching out to the entire Jewish world was the wisest course of action for the Modern Orthodox to pursue at this moment in European Jewish history.

It happened once, in 1881, that Hildesheimer was asked whether boys could be allowed to study with uncovered heads in a Jewish school. The school, located in Vienna and sponsored by the Jewish community, forbade headcoverings "on sanitary grounds." Hildesheimer recognized, of course, that the ostensible reason given for the prohibition on headcoverings was ridiculous; he assumed that the majority of the board which had issued the ruling was either Reform or secular. While he admitted that skullcaps were not mandated by Jewish law, he insisted that tradition expected males to wear them while eating, praying, or studying holy texts. He went on: as the wearing of the headcovering had become, by this point in Jewish history, a universally observed Jewish custom, the tradition should continue to be observed. Nevertheless, and for our purposes this is most significant, Hildesheimer was not primarily concerned with whether the boys wore a headcovering while studying. Instead, Hildesheimer maintained, the issue which concerned him most was that Orthodox children were obviously attending school where the majority, or at least a sizable minority, of students were non-Orthodox and non-observant. He feared the influences such children would have on their Orthodox peers and contended that it would be better for the Orthodox parents to remove their children from such an educational institution. Hildesheimer clearly believed that if the modern Orthodox were to achieve religious authority, they had to consolidate their strength in their own community rather than reach out to the larger one. He comprehended the boundaries of Orthodox religious influence in the general Jewish community in which he lived.[57]

This interpretation was underscored by another event three years later. On Octover 25, 1884, a committee of Hovevei Tsiyon in Warsaw sent Hildesheimer a telegram urging him to attend their forthcoming convention in Kattowitz, Austrian Poland, on November 6. The committee felt that Hildesheimer's attendance at the conference would aid in gaining both financial and ideological support from Orthodox and German Jews.[58] Despite his sympathy for their cause, Hildesheimer declined this particular invitation. In a letter to Leon Pinsker, he claimed that advancing age and a heavy workload made his attendance impossible, but clearly it was his own sectarian religious stance which dictated his absence from the conference. On the one hand, Hildesheimer objected to the fact that the conference was being co-sponsored by the B'nai B'rith lodge in Kattowitz. Though a member of the Berlin lodge, he claimed that the members of the Kattowitz chapter were blatantly anti-religious.[59] As Hildesheimer saw the rebuilding of the Land of Israel in religious terms, he considered it inappropriate to lend formal support to the Kattowitz gathering and even rejected Pinsker's effort to persuade him to become an honorary member of the committee.[60] It is apparent, however, that this decision on Hildesheimer's part was also grounded in a judgment he made about his ability to exercise influential religious authority among the Jews of Germany, an ability he perceived as limited on account of his religious sectarianism. Hildesheimer pointed out to Pinsker that his influence on the great bulk of German Jews on an issue such as this was minimal. His support of the committee, he said, would not aid significantly in securing either additional financial or intellectual support for the Zionist organization. As he wrote, "You are certainly wrong if you believe that my influence on this question is in general effective with my co-religionists."[61] His inability to exercise influential religious authority among German Jews in this matter does not appear to have disturbed him.

The final contours of Hildesheimer's policy toward other religious groups in the contemporary Jewish commuinity can be seen in his position regarding "secession." Hildesheimer, it will be recalled, had, in 1847, opposed Reform "secession" from the general Jewish community as proposed by Philippson and the Reformers. At that juncture he had believed in the possibility of Orthodox hegemony over the entire Jewish community. In 1869, however, by accepting the post of rabbi of Congregation Adass Jisroel in Berlin, Hildesheimer demonstrated that his religious sectarianism had led him to believe it advisable for the Orthodox to create their own religious institutions apart from the potential obstructions posed by a Reform minority in the general Jewish community. Secondly, in 1875, Hildesheimer supported Samson Raphael Hirsch in his efforts to have the Prussian Parliament pass a law of secession which would permit Orthodox Jews and others to secede from and thereby no longer pay taxes to the general Jewish community. On July 27, 1876, the law was passed and Hildesheimer was instrumental in its passage. In laboring on its behalf, Hildesheimer stated, "The gulf between the adherents of traditional Judaism and its religious faith is at least as deep and wide as in any other religious faith; in fact, it is larger than in most and much bigger than what is permitted by law."[62] Hildesheimer's religious sectarianism thus persuaded him to adopt a position of separation from other Jewish religious groups in nineteenth century Germany and provided a paradigm for Modern Jewish Orthodoxy in the contemporary world.

Nevertheless, it is vital to emphasize that Hildesheimer, throughout this period, retained his churchlike posture in regard to contemporary Western culture. He supported the education of girls in Jewish religious subjects, an innovation in the context of the nineteenth century;[63] he supported secular education for Jewish students,[64] remained sensitive to nineteenth century German aesthetic standards,[65] was eager to participate in the political process of the modern world,[66] and remained concerned over how Orthodoxy was perceived by acculturated members of the German Jewish community.[67] In short, his brand of Jewish Orthodoxy might be described as one "of low tension with the social environment." Like the Judaism of the Reformers, his Orthodoxy could clearly be labelled a church in regard to this important characteristic. Yet, because of his experiences in the latter part of the century, Hildesheimer knew that Orthodoxy could not maintain its hegemony over the total Jewish community in Central Europe. Indeed, his own brand of Modern Orthodoxy was destined to be uninfluential among Orthodox Jews who rejected the worth of secular culture. Consequently, as has been seen, Hildesheimer -- because of the dual nature of his approach to Western culture (which was churchlike) and Jewish religious dogma (which was sectarian) -- considered it best to appeal only to those Jews who simultaneously affirmed both the Tradition (as interpreted by the Modern Orthodox) and the value of Western culture.

Perhaps the most accurate statement which reflects the dual nature of the Hildesheimer position is to be found in a description which Samuel Montagu offered of Hildesheimer himself. In a letter addressed to Benjamin Hirsch, Hildesheimer's nephew, on December 8, 1877, Montagu, one of the most prominent and richest Jews in England, wrote:

> I had the pleasure of seeing your esteemed uncle, Dr. Hildesheimer, several times. I am glad to make the acquaintance of so worthy a man and so renowned a scholar. I was pleased to find that he holds such liberal ideas in secular matters at the same time being perfectly Orthodox in religion and strictly observing all our holy laws.[68]

Such testimony quite accurately reflects Hildesheimer's persona and explains why Hildesheimer succeeded quite remarkably in his program to achieve Orthodox religious authority among certain segments of an acculturated German Jewry. It also explains the limitations of his influence and why it was that Hildesheimer assumed a sectarian stance in regard to non-Orthodox religious bodies in Judaism.

Afterword

In looking at Hildesheimer and Modern Orthodoxy through the lens of church-sect theory, we see, on the one hand, the limitations of the theory in its classical form. For, as Hildesheimer illustrates, a religious movement can be "in low tension with the social environment," and, simultaneously, be highly dogmatic in regard to creed, preferring separation from other groups to a compromise of principles -- a pronounceably sectarian quality. It is tempting to label Modern Orthodoxy an "anomaly" among religious movements, but it would be more illuminating to employ Liebman's insight about the double bind in which modernity places Judaism and to state that a religious movement like Modern Jewish Orthodoxy can take one stance consistent with its attitude toward secular society and another position which is consistent with its program regarding Jewish society. In fact, this, as we have seen, was the case with Hildesheimer and Modern Jewish Orthodoxy. As such, the employment of church-sect theory in this modified form, aids in clarifying the study of Modern Jewish Orthodoxy in particular and holds promise as a heuristic device for understanding the nature of the modern Jewish response to the general challenge of the modern world.

JEWS AND SOUTHERNERS: THE PRISM OF LITERATURE

Stephen J. Whitfield
Brandeis University

Consider the career of an American writer who was born in 1923, flew numerous combat missions during the Second World War, and then returned home to attend college and receive a master's degree in literature. After teaching the subject he entered advertising before his writing on the side brought acclaim and success. If this outline of an author's career sounds vaguely familiar, it may be because it has emerged in duplicate. Two writers fit its profile: James Dickey and Joseph Heller. How they differ, however, is both more interesting and more suggestive of the cultural imperatives that distinguish Southern Gentiles from Jewish Americans. Such contrasts may provide important evidence of the recalcitrance and resilience of Jewish identity, highlighted against the most historically intolerant, most thoroughly Protestant part of American society.

Dickey's poetry exerts its power through its descriptiveness. For him the poet is above all an observer, "someone who notices and is enormously taken by things that somebody else would walk by." Although Dickey himself was born in Atlanta, rather than in the countryside, he believes that the best Southern verse has been inspired not by its people but by its landscape. Therefore, the supreme subject for the contemporary poet, he argues, is "dying nature," because "the animals are going, the trees are going, the flowers are going, everything is going." That is the fear with which he imbues the character of Lewis in _Deliverance_ (1970). Dickey's only novel taps a sense of the disappearance of the natural order before the inexorable intrusion of industrial "progress." Of course the tale also certifies the achievement of manhood in the wilderness, which imposes tests of courage that contemporary society ordinarily forsakes. Its setting is nature rather than society, its characters are men without women, and it is streaked with violence. That is why one critic shrewdly observed that Dickey has composed the kind of book Norman Mailer has tried in vain to write -- the ultimate Wasp novel, the fiction of Esau. It might also be added that, though right-wing political views have been attributed to Dickey, he denies harboring such opinions and insists that he holds no explicit political stance whatsoever.[1]

The contrast with Heller is illuminating. For he admits that he cannot write descriptive passages in his novels, that the detailed observation of the environment is outside his range. Unlike Dickey, Heller writes no poetry and lacks a lyrical gift. Instead his novels are thick with psychological nuance and convolution, which are often endowed with a comic twist lacking in Dickey's work. The milieu of Heller's fiction is urban (he was born in Brooklyn), or bureaucratic, or both. Oddly enough, he claims that he cannot write a novel until an opening sentence occurs to him, which gives added significance to what was initially intended to be the opening of Something Happened: "In the office in which I work, there are four people of whom I am afraid. Each of these four people is afraid of five people." That passage became the opening of the second section of the novel, whose final draft began as follows: "I get the willies when I see closed doors." The stance of the novels is therefore one of radical alienation. It is not implausible to believe that Heller had himself in mind when, in Catch-22 (1961), the psychiatrist, Major Sanderson, tells John Yossarian: "You have a morbid aversion to dying . . . And you don't like bigots, bullies, snobs or hypocrites . . . You're antagonistic to the idea of being exploited, degraded, humiliated or deceived."[2] In the original draft of Heller's most celebrated novel, the protagonist was a Jew, but became an Assyrian American in the final version -- even as the protagonist of Philip Roth's The Great American Novel, "the greatest rookie of all time," is Gil Gamesh, a Babylonian and another exotic outsider. The human virtue that is most problematic in Catch-22 is not courage but justice, and what matters to its hero is not the capacity to kill but the struggle to avoid being killed. Though Catch-22 is a war novel, it reveals no interest in bravery.

Here some generalizations may be introduced. Southern whites have often been initiated into manhood through the ritual of the hunt; and from the earliest regional writers through Faulkner, the bear hunt has symbolized the passage into adulthood. (This theme was ludicrously misappropriated in Mailer's last attempt at the Wasp novel, Why Are We in Vietnam? [1967]). By contrast Jews have historically felt an aversion for such sport and have experienced little fondness for hound dogs going into a frenzy. Coursing through the works of many

Jewish writers of the twentieth century, from Kafka through Heller, is the persistent sense of being hunted, beleaguered, vulnerable.

The Southerner has typically lived on farms or in small towns and has been deeply attached to the soil and to his roots. His sense of place and locale has seemed almost visceral, and his association with the land has formed bonds that other Americans undoubtedly find eccentric. A "mournful, discommoded, fundamentally displaced tone . . . came to Southerners when they moved even from their own small town to the next," Mailer has noticed. "No one suffered so much as Southerners with uprooting."[3] So aware have Southern writers been of their setting that such knowledge can become intrusive. For instance, in William Styron's The Confessions of Nat Turner (1967), lush descriptions of the land and the climate are provided by the narrator, whose historical model -- the real Nat Turner -- would surely have had much else to worry about.

By contrast the Jews have been primarily an urban people, even in Russia'a Pale of Settlement at the end of the nineteenth century. Long prohibited from owning land, they became accustomed to being walkers -- and talkers -- in the city. Long despised as pariahs, they experienced fully the meaning of displacement. Observation of the natural world -- its trees and flowers, animals and birds -- has been rarely recorded by Jewish writers. Notice the mistake that even Isaac Bashevis Singer made when, in being introduced to a Poe scholar at the University of Buffalo, he gushingly hailed Poe as "a genius . . . . But the poem about the crow is overrated." As for those small towns from which Southerners hated to be detached, Gertrude Stein can for once be taken as representative of many other Jews when she remarked of such hamlets: "When you go there, there is no there there." Even in the modern South outside of Florida, about two-thirds of all Jews live in cities whose population is greater than 250,000. Ironically enough the Jewish experience of exile and estrangement, their habituation in cities and therefore early confrontation with modernity may today make them less disoriented in the region than natives. John Bickerson "Binx" Boling, the New Orleans stockbroker of Walker Percy's National Book Award-winning The Moviegoer, asserts: "I am more Jewish than the Jews I know. They are more at home than I am. I accept my exile."[4] But for most Jews, at least until recently, the paradigm of their experience has been not brotherhood but "otherhood," often in the South itself.

Both Southerners and Jews have been haunted by the past and burdened by their histories. They have sensed that they were somehow special, different. But the lessons that they have absorbed from the past have been quite different. William Faulkner's resonant reverie bears quotation: "For every Southern boy fourteen years old, not once but whenever he wants it, there is the instant when it's still not two o'clock on that July afternoon in 1863, the brigades are in position behind the rail fence, the guns are laid and ready in the woods, and the furled flags are already loosened to break out and Pickett himself [is] . . . is waiting for Longstreet to give the word and it's all in the balance, it hasn't happened yet . . . "[5] Here then are the contours of a community, sealed in warfare, in defeat, in cussedness, in fantasy. The special moment of the Jews has not been military, but moral. Their history stretches back ever so sinuously and mysteriously, at least as far back as the giving of the law on Mount Sinai, where -- according to Midrashic legend -- all Jews -- past, present, future -- were present. Here the destiny of a people was forged that had promised to live according to the yoke of ethical monotheism, chosen to assume special moral responsibilities, to be a kingdom of priests and a holy people. Its demands -- and its memories -- are therefore quite distinctive, and quite long. "I have been a Jew for four thousand years," Rabbi Stephen S. Wise wrote in 1939. "I have been an American for sixty-four years."[6]

Perhaps even more than other Americans, Southerners regarded positive law as an impediment. The historian Daniel J. Boorstin, born in Atlanta, where his father had been involved in the defense of Leo Frank, has stressed the fidelity of the gentlemen of the Old South to the code duello.[7] For these children of pride, conflicts were to be resolved on the field on honor, not in a court of law. The only equality which many white Southerners have been inclined to affirm was supplied by Colonel Colt, and the character ideal they tried to emulate was emotional rather than rational. That character could become something explosive and dangerous, rich in red-clay craziness. The tradition that emerged was so immoderate that only the violent bear it away. Southerners have long acknowledged their bellicosity, and circulated a story about former Confederate general Robert Toombs, rushing to the telegraph office to hear the news of the great Chicago fire of 1871. Toombs passed on to his fellow Georgians the report that the city was taking all

possible protective measures to prevent the spread of the flames
and then added: "But the wind is in our favor." When Willie
Morris of Yazoo, Mississippi came to New York to find a job
among the city's publishers and editors, expecting to tell them
that Willie Boy is here, he was treated with such indifference
and condescension by Jason Epstein at Random House that Morris
began to get angry: "A slow Mississippi boil was beginning to
rise north from my guts, a physical presence that had always
warned me . . . to beware of my heritage of violence, bloodshed,
and spur-of-the-moment mayhem." But Morris resisted the desire
for defenestration, the impulse to hurl "this little man out of
a second-story window into a courtyard." Even the journalist
Robert Sherrill, born in Frogtown, Georgia (which no longer
exists), could doubt, after brilliantly indicting the national
cult of guns, whether reform is possible. For even in himself
he concedes that "those genes that came over to supply labor for
Oglethorpe's debtor colony keep responding the wrong way."
During a literary quarrel in the late 1940's, the poet Allen
Tate, author of "Ode to the Confederate Dead," challenged an
editor of Partisan Review to a duel.[8] That is, in part, how
Southerners have defined themselves.

Here again the contrast with Jewish values is striking.
Whatever the requirements of Realpolitik within which the state
of Israel has felt constrained to operate for its survival, the
ideal of shalom , of peace, has remained the essence of Jewish
aspiration. Antagonism to military values, which are part of
European Jewish folklore, made the passage to the New World as
well. One example is Irving Berlin's "Good Bye Becky Cohen,"
popular on the old East Side. When Becky's boy friend goes off
to war, she replies: "What, fight for nothing/Where's the
percentage in that?/No, you better mind your store/Let McCarthy
go to war."[9] Civilian life has been far preferable; and for
the sake of prudence, the Jews have generally avoided heroism.
Lionel Trilling observed that "the Rabbis, in speaking of
virtue, never mention the virtue of courage, which Aristotle
regarded as basic to the heroic character. The indifference of
the Rabbis to the idea of courage is the more remarkable in that
they knew that many of their number would die for their faith."
Perhaps no other ethnic group would tell a joke about itself or
find its truth so piercing, as in the tale of the two Jews lined
up against the wall to be shot. When one of them demands from
the leader of the firing squad a final cigarette, the other Jew
whispers to him: "Shhhh, don't make trouble." Here is no ideal

of unreconstructed ferocity, no cult of violent response to
adversity or authority. After slapping and kicking an American
soldier in a military hospital in Sicily in 1943, General George
S. Patton, a Virginian, announced: "There's no such thing as
shell shock. It's an invention of the Jews."[10]

Because the Southern character ideal has been emotional,
Ellen Glasgow could write of the protagonist of her novel
Virginia: "She was capable of dying for an idea, but not of
conceiving one." Yet the region had not always been H. L.
Mencken's Sahara of the Bozart; and most of the political ideas
that sparked the American Revolution and the subsequent creation
of the republic had been formulated in Glasgow's own state of
Virginia. (Indeed President Kennedy once engaged in justifiable
hyperbole when, in welcoming America's Nobel Prize winners to
the White House, he lauded "the most extraordinary collection of
talent, of human knowledge, that has ever gather together at the
White House, with the possible exception of when Thomas
Jefferson dined alone.") Nevertheless the intellectual power of
the Old South waned quickly enough, and has never been
replenished. Henry Adams generalized boldly from his
association at Harvard College with the son of Robert E. Lee:
"The Southerner had no mind; he had temperament. He was not a
scholar; he had no intellectual training, he could not analyze
an idea, and he could not even conceive of admitting two."[11]
Particularly in our century many very talented writers have
resisted the temptation to live and die in Dixie. One of the
problems in defining who Southern writers are is their
inclination in many cases to leave the region. The anabasis
(going North) of Tate, Styron, Thomas Wolfe, Tom Wolfe, Stark
Young, Joseph Wood Krutch, James Agee, Robert Penn Warren,
Carson McCullers, Truman Capote, C. Vann Woodward, and others,
including major black writers, has long threatened to lend
credence to the American intellectuals' riddle: what is the
difference between the South and yoghurt? Answer: yoghurt has
an active culture. Even today Robert Penn Warren's home county
in Kentucky lacks a public library and bookmobile.[12]

The Jewish character ideal has stressed self-control rather
than the expression of instinct; it has promoted self-discipline
rather than spontaneity of emotion. Moderation, discretion,
continence, and even resignation were supposed to be the way one
responded to the bad luck which, as the proverb went, could
always find a Jew. And beginning with Spinoza, who invested
thought with moral passion and who bore a most ambiguous

relationship to his "coreligionists," the contribution of the
Jews to Western civilization in the modern era is far out of
proportion to their numbers. This phenomenon needs no
embroidery here. But as Pasternak's Lara says to Dr. Zhivago,
"If you do intellectual work of any kind and live in a town as
we do, half of your friends are bound to be Jews." Such
circumstances have their equivalents in the United States as
well. "There wouldn't be any active American culture now
without the Jewish element," Robert Lowell commented in 1964.
"They are small in numbers, but they're a leaven that changes
the whole intellectual world of America. It's a painful reality
that a minority should have such liveliness and vigor. You're
sort of at a loss why the rest of the country doesn't equal
that."[13] What has been bequeathed to America's Jews is a
tradition whose rationalism and skepticism, whose critical
intensity and creative dissidence cannot easily be squared with
what Southerners find most compelling and most vivid in their
own heritage.

Differences in literary expression have escaped the
attention of all but a couple of critics. One of the few
scholars who has attempted to assess, however briefly, the
divergent paths of Southern and Jewish writers is one who is
both, Louis D. Rubin. University Distinguished Professor of
English at Chapel Hill, Rubin has noted that both Southerners
and Jews are "ancestor-conscious." They are "strong on familial
ties, and not thoroughly assimilated into the mainstream of
modern American life." Yet Rubin added that the central
character in the typical American Jewish novel "accepts the
practical conditions and values of the dominant culture, which
is . . . largely Protestant . . . But at the same time he feels
a bit uneasy in it, cannot quite make entire sense of it, and so
refuses to be engulfed in and fully defined by it." Rubin's
view is echoed by Irving Howe, the author of a fairly early and
enthusiastic study of Faulkner, though better known as the
elegiast of the World of Our Fathers (1976). The Southerner,
Howe argues, has of course been a Christian, and therefore the
condition of being an outsider is "a partial and temporary one,
by now almost at an end." The Jew, however, cannot entirely
escape the sense of distinctiveness, which historical memory has
imposed, no matter how decisively religion has gone into eclipse
and no matter how fully Western civilization has become
secularized. The vestigial claims of the past are too powerful,
Howe has insisted, implying that some spirit of estrangement is

inevitable for the Jewish writer.[14]   The poet Delmore Schwartz
tried to rebut the critical claim that he was trying to be a
second T. S. Eliot by arguing that Eliot could not have been
"motivated by the alienation which only a Jew can suffer, and
use, as a cripple uses his weakness in order to beg."[15]
Reuben Warshovsky, the character of the New York labor organizer
played by Ron Liebman in the film Norma Rae (1979), is more
gnomic. An intruder in the dust, he is the first Jew that the
eponymous Carolina textile worker played by Sally Field has ever
seen. As they become friends, she wonders what makes the Jews
different, since they don't seem to be. Warshovsky, her
political and cultural Pygmalion, replies: "History."

    That experience is something that, paradoxically, Southern
whites and blacks have in common. When Willie Morris settled in
New York and was appointed editor of Harper's, he discovered
less of a bond with New York's predominantly Jewish literati
than with certain black writers like Ralph Ellison and Albert
Murray. Although Morris had been born and raised in a
segregated town, they "shared the same easy-going conversation;
the casual talk and the telling of stories, in the Southern
verbal jam-session way; the sense of family and the past and
people out of the past; the congenial social manner and the
mischievous laughter . . . " Morris added to this list a common
"love of the American language in its accuracy and vividness and
simplicity; the obsession with the sensual experience of America
in all its extravagance and diversity; the love of animals and
sports, of the outdoors and sour mash; the distrust . . . of
certain manifestations of Eastern intellectualism . . ." In the
extensive writing of American Jews, it it impossible to find any
nostalgia for the meal that the Morrises, the Ellisons and the
Murrays enjoyed one New Year's Day in Harlem: collard greens,
ham-hocks, black-eyed peas, cornbread and bourbon.[16]

    Morris does not mention the Christian origins which they
shared, but that too should be remarked upon, if only in
passing. Gentile attitudes toward Jews have historically been
shaped by religious doctrines. It should not be too surprising
that Southern Baptists whom sociologists interviewed in
California for the Anti-Defamation League in the early 1960's
were more likely than members of any other denomination to
believe that no salvation outside of Jesus is possible. Only
conversion to Christianity could therefore avoid the danger of
damnation; and Eli Evans, a Southern Jew who also made the trek
north, has recalled how widespread was the Southern Jewish

anticipation of meeting proselytizers sincerely anxious to save souls.[17] In the United States today, it is not often realized that about a quarter of all evangelicals are blacks, though the impact of Protestantism upon the black imagination is a staple of historical and sociological discourse.

Yet even though the South is often depicted as a God-intoxicated region, very few traces of religiously-inspired anti-Semitism can be found in its literature. Carson McCullers' The Ballad of the Sad Cafe (1943) is hardly to be read as a tale of realistic exactitude, but it is set in a Southern mill town where "the soul rots with boredom." There the grotesques and freaks who inhabit the village have taken delight in harassing one Morris Finestein, "a quick, skipping little Jew who cried if you called him Christkiller, and ate light bread and canned salmon every day." Finestein had departed after a calamity; but ever since, "if a man were prissy in any way, or if a man ever wept, he was known as a Morris Finestein." The author's detestation of such cruelty is clear enough, however, even out of context.[18] When Richard Wright was growing up in Elaine, Arkansas, the first Jew he ever saw was the proprietor of a grocery store, just as the grocery store that the Wingfields patronize in Tennessee Williams' The Glass Menagerie (1945) is Garfinkel's. But in Wright's autobiography he recorded the hostility that was triggered: "All of us black people who lived in the neighborhood hated Jews, not because they exploited us, but because we had been taught at home and in Sunday School that Jews were 'Christ killers.'" Though Wright believed that such hatred "was bred in us from childhood . . . it was part of our cultural heritage," no empirical evidence has yet sustained the view that such anti-Semitism was rampant among Southern blacks -- nor among whites either.[19]

A comparison with blacks further documents how much more deeply the spirit of alienation has sunk among Jews than among Southerners. Stripped of all but the residue of their African origins, they became native sons. Their resilience, inventiveness, and adaptability have been exhibited within one culture; and blacks have often asked only to be included in a society that would grant them equality and dignity. Names are a giveaway. When Booker T. Washington, having been born in slavery, went to public school for the first time, he did not know that he had a surname. So he bestowed upon himself that of the father of his country, even though the first President had been a slaveholder. When historian John Hope Franklin's grandfather, a runaway slave, got north, he assumed the surname of Benjamin Franklin, among the most conservative of the Founders.[20] And Ellison himself is named Ralph Waldo, in honor of the poet who is far better known for his sagacity than his subversiveness.

The Jews have generally identified more closely with Americans who represented either dissidence or a fuller expression of the democratic experiment. One immigrant family, the Rostows, named their sons after Walt Whitman and Eugene V. Debs (which is why the radio station of the Jewish Daily Forward in New York was called WEVD). The eminent explicator of Puritanism and translator of Yiddish literature, Sacvan Bercovitch, is named after Sacco and Vanzetti. When little Alexander Portnoy is asked which Americans in history he most admires, he replies: Thomas Paine and Abraham Lincoln (not Franklin or Washington). The status of the outsider still sometimes clings to the Jew. Even though the New Orleans philanthropist Judah Touro subscribed half of the funds to erect the Bunker Hill monument, even though the Levy family rescued Monticello from ruin a century ago, the sense of Jews as not quite belonging is illustrated in F. Scott Fitzgerald's The Last Tycoon (1941). Narrated by a movie producer's daughter, Celia Brady, the novel opens in Nashville, which is visited by a Jew who is also in the movie business: "He had come a long way from some ghetto to present himself at that raw shrine. Manny Schwartz and Andrew Jackson -- it was hard to say them in the same sentence."[21] A friend of mine, a graduate student from Chicago who was recently en route to do research on ante-bellum Southern Protestantism, went into a store in Montreat, North Carolina. He was almost immediately asked: "Are you Jewish?" My friend was taken a little aback, wondering if he'd indeed run into a co-religionist, and replied: "Yes, are you?" There was a pause, and then the manager replied: "No, I'm an American." There, on native grounds, the manager probably would not have said that to a black, who could not have been perceived as a stranger in the same way.

Part of the difference may well be, in literary terms, noticeable through language, as Willie Morris has written. Already at Tuskegee in the 1930s, with the area aflame with the scandal of the Scottsboro trial, Ellison was absorbed in Faulkner's prose. It is no secret that Southerners have long prided themselves on their rhetorical skills, on their flair for oratory and indeed orotundity. (Visiting New Orleans in 1960,

the New York journalist Adolph Joseph Liebling attempted to get
outside the W. J. Cash nexus by remarking that the 1941 classic
should have been entitled "The Mouth of the South.") Southern
writers have often considered themselves the legatees of
Shakespeare's ripeness and of the stateliness of the King James
version. Katherine Anne Porter, who was born in Texas and
raised in Louisiana, once insisted: "We are in the direct,
legitimate line, we are people based in English as our mother
tongue, and we do not abuse it or misuse it, and when we speak a
word, we know what it means. These others," she commented,
without naming names, "have fallen into a curious kind of argot,
more or less originating in New York, a deadly mixture of
academic, guttersnipe, gangster, fake-Yiddish, and dull old
wornout dirty words -- an appalling bankruptcy in language, as
if they hate English and are trying to destroy it along with all
other living things they touch."[22] Class dismissed. But she
also showed prescience, since Portnoy's Complaint was not to be
published until four years later. Porter's sensibility, with
its stress upon historical fidelity and normative elegance,
could not accommodate the kind of writing that has by now
quickened the beat of the American idiom, enlarging its
possibilities for paradox and incongruity and irony. Our
national tongue is not only more salty but also more expressive
and more resourceful, for that "fake-Yiddish" has put a spin on
our vernacular and sent it hopping into those realms of fiction
where the language renews itself.

That is probably why the success of the Southern literary
renascence has yielded, in the opinion of many observers, to
Jewish writing. "The most dramatic change in the American
literary situation," Styron remarked in 1971, "has been the
efflorescence of Jewish writers in all fields . . . There have
been occasions when upon reading an issue of the New York Times
Book Review I have gained the impression that all the new and
interesting novelists were Jews." He added that the cause has
undoubtedly been in part due to "the shift in America from the
pastoral, small-town life style to the urban equivalent with its
weird and singular frights and tensions. They in turn comprise
such a setup for the Jewish sensibility: that comic awareness
so exquisitely poised between hilarity and anguish which seems
the perfect literary foil for the monstrousness of life in the
big cities."[23]

Such observations have become commonplace. But some
qualifications are surely in order. One is that "schools" are

categories that include the very talented and the less so, those
who demonstrate their membership in the pantheon of art and
those who are simply gate-crashers. Moreover it is too easy to
exaggerate the luster of earlier Southern fiction and poetry.
In the Gutenberg galaxy that includes American literature in
this century, Faulkner is the only supernova, the only one to
light up the sky over Stockholm. As the sole owner and
proprietor of Yoknapatawpha County, he alone belongs to the
world, having managed to leave behind an oeuvre that does not
betray the highest expectations and consolations of art. If,
among the nineteenth century figures, Poe and Twain are not
included in the classification of Southern writers, then even
the term "renascence" is something of a misnomer. For similar
literary power was not exhibited by those few authors still
remembered today, like George Washington Cable, a liberal who
went into Northern exile; Kate Chopin, only recently
rediscovered because of one slender but moving tale; and O.
Henry, whose name is preserved -- in an increasingly
analphabetic age -- as a candy bar. These are not major
writers, even though they may be superior to other regions'
literary figures. It is also entirely false to assume that
Southern literature is burned out, though some of its earlier
stars -- most notably Thomas Wolfe -- now appear much less
luminous.

The same warnings apply to any critical judgements of Jewish
writers. They form even less of a cohesive school, and are even
more various, than Southerners. To try to find similarities
between those Saul Bellow has nicknamed the Hart, Schaffner and
Marx of Jewish letters (himself, Bernard Malamud and Philip
Roth) and such disparate writers of Jewish birth as Gertrude
Stein, Susan Sontag, Chaim Potok, S. J. Perelman, Tillie Olsen,
Paul Goodman, and Alan Friedman -- to say nothing of such
half-Jews as J. D. Salinger and Dorothy Parker, or of Isaac
Bashevis Singer, the only American winner of the Nobel Prize for
Literature whose books have to be translated into English -- is
to realize that here is no monolithic group, no kosher nostra.
No Faulkner has emerged among them as pre-eminent, as
authoritative enough to generate the anxiety of influence.

If they share a primary topic of interest at all, which is
doubtful, it may well be the family romance. For many of them
have understood that the family has been the secret of cultural
transmission, the Jewish double helix that codifies and
replicates the historic destiny of an ancient people. At least

until the recent phase of the history of American Jews, their
English may have been broken, but their homes were not. The
family romance, with all the loyalty that it engendered and all
the rage that it stirred, has been so pervasive and irresistible
a theme that Roth's utterly unpleasant academic poet, Ralph
Baumgarten, perversely refuses to write about his family. "Can
you actually get worked up over another son and another daughter
and another mother and another father driving each other nuts?"
he asks David Kepesh, Roth's "professor of desire." "All that
loving; all the hating; all those meals. And don't forget the
menschlichkeit. And the baffled quest for dignity. Oh, and the
goodness . . . I understand somebody has just published a whole
book on our Jewish literature of goodness" -- perhaps an
allusion to the dissertation Josephine Z. Knopp published on The
Trial of Judaism in Contemporary Jewish Writing (1975).
Baumgarten continues, ever so slyly: "I expect any day to read
. . . an article by some good old boy from Vanderbilt on
hospitality in the Southern novel: 'Make Yourself at Home: The
Theme of Hospitality in Faulkner's "A Rose for Emily."'"[24]
Few Jewish writers seem to have followed Baumgarten's example,
since such themes are virtually the only story most of them
know. Yet Irving Howe has identified only one masterpiece so
far on the shelves of American Jewish novels: Henry Roth's
dissection of an immigrant family, Call It Sleep (1934).[25]
Such a judgment, while probably erring on the side of severity,
nevertheless provides a useful corrective to the praise that has
been showered on talents which are assumed to be formidable
because they were burnished in Flatbush or in the Delta, where
such writers presumably got a contact high from proximity to
serious artists.

Why these two literatures became so pertinent has not been
examined in any systematic way. Howe has argued that both have
emerged when the doom of the cultures they described had already
been sealed. Only when the power of a culture has evaporated,
he speculates, can it be understood adequately to be transmuted
into art. For "such a moment of high self-consciousness offers
writers the advantages of an inescapable subject: the judgment,
affection and hatred they bring to bear upon the remembered
world of their youth, and the costs exacted by their struggle to
tear themselves away." Thus the critic and story-teller Isaac
Rosenfeld could assert that Faulkner's best work was not written
"about the South, but over it, over its dead body, in a moment
of complete triumph."[26] Such an interpretation would not

apply to <u>The White Rose of Memphis</u>, written by his
great-grandfather, Col. William Falkner.

Yet this formulation, though it has merit, is not entirely
satisfactory. In modern times, it has often been observed, the
only constant is change; and yet every age of transition does
not produce literature of permanent excellence. The Old South
also died, and yet the pebbles thrown on its grave could not be
transformed into radiant and enduring literature. Certainly
some of the best Southern literati, like Faulkner, Warren and
Tate, have been endowed with an historical consciousness. Their
work has civic spirit, which does not mean that it produced
larger voter turnouts but that it made meaningful connections
between private experience and communal pressures. Yet others
who contributed to the distinction associated with Southern
literary life have lacked that sense of a disintegrating
culture. These would include not only several women but also
Agee and Wolfe, who are not strictly speaking regionalists at
all and who may therefore be regarded as lapsed Southerners.

The Jewish authors are likewise so varied that Howe's
generalization cannot possibly embrace them all, unless the
sense of an ending is what itself defines the Jewish writer.
Some of them can scarcely be connected to the Eastern Europe
from which most American Jews have stemmed; many have only the
faintest inkling of the religious texture of Judaism; many do
not write about the Jewish condition at all. For virtually all
modern intellectuals, God is an imaginary character whose
absence is occasionally missed. The relationship of its
intellectuals to a people historically defined by its ethical
monotheism is therefore problematic, and may well instigate the
formulation of an artistic response. It is curious however that
earlier beliefs in the imminent end of the Jewish religion or
people did not stimulate the release of comparable literary
expressiveness. "There was hardly a generation in the Diaspora
period which did not consider itself the final link in Israel's
chain," one Judaic scholar has written in an essay ironically
entitled "Israel, the Ever-Dying People." For "each generation
grieved not only for itself but also for the great past which
was going to disappear forever, as well as for the future of
unborn generations who would never see the light of day."[27]
Yet despite the continual fears that the vital signs of group
life were flickering, only since the Second World War have
Jewish writers conspicuously emerged to confront what supposedly
remained of a once-vibrant culture. Howe's conjecture does not

account for the particular moment in which the ambivalence of post-religious Jews shaped itself into literature worthy of attracting national attention.

Moreover the impact of a dying tradition should have encouraged the literature of Southern Jews, in whom the twentieth century experience of dislocation and disinheritance should have been compounded. The disjunctions and incongruities in being both Southern and Jewish ought to have created many more serious writers than in fact can be identified. The conflicting values and incompatible ideals which could not be logically resolved might at least have been artistically formulated. This has not yet occurred.

Yet out of such dissonance literature is supposed to flourish. Southerners and Jews are supposed to be intoxicated with words, and yet few Southern Jews have quarreled enough within themselves to create imaginative literature of incontrovertible value. They have largely been silent. To be sure the first book of verse published by a Jew in the United States was Fancy's Sketch Book (1833), by Penina Moise of Charleston. But she may be more interesting for being first, the Jewish equivalent of Anne Bradstreet or Phyllis Wheatley; and those familiar with her work concede that she was not blessed with poetic gifts.[28] She is omitted from the Bibliographic Guide to the Study of Southern Literature, whose only writer of Jewish origin is Lillian Hellman, of New Orleans, of whom more later. There has been an occasional undistinguished novel (Ronald Bern's The Legacy) and play (Gus Weill's To Bury a Cousin), in which good intentions outstrip the capacity to create vibrancy and complexity. There have been historical novels about Southern Jews, like Judah P. Benjamin (Gray Fox) and Leo Frank (Member of the Tribe) -- but these were not written by Southern Jews. There have been minor Jewish novelists raised in the South, like Ludwig Lewisohn; but his work was mostly apologetic and apodictic. There have been intellectuals born or raised in the South -- journalists, historians, sociologists. But with some very recent exceptions -- Rubin's Surfaces of a Diamond, Roy Hoffman's Almost Family, Ellen Monsky's Midnight Suppers -- they have not composed novels. Like Sebastian Venable in Suddenly Last Summer, who every summer went away to compose his summer poem, Southern Jews have not been productive writers.

Such silence merits reflection. Perhaps so many Jews have been busy minding the store that they could not contribute to

the mind of the South.   The rule that writing is a full-time
occupation allows for only a few exceptions; it is too
exorbitant in its demands to allow much room for maneuver.
Nevertheless what is odd is that the class of businessmen and
store-keepers produced so few offspring with creative and
intellectual gifts, although this was the class that produced a
vibrant Jewish intelligentsia in Europe and often in the North.
Nor is demography an absolute impediment, for sometimes a
distinctively minority community can blossom with literature of
international importance.   The Protestant middle class of
Dublin, for instance, produced Shaw, Wilde, Yeats and Beckett;
and either by birth or through conversion, Catholicism has
attracted Walker Percy, Allen Tate and Flannery O'Connor, even
though few Southerners subscribe to that faith.

It would even be possible to argue that the Jewish community
in the South has produced enough fascinating, striking,
conspicuous and even exotic characters to serve as incentives to
the imagination.   Perhaps none has been as strange as Two-Gun
Cohen, who was the bodyguard of Sun Yat-sen.   But consider the
doctors (like the surgeon general of the Confederacy; or the
father of Bernard Baruch, who rode with the Ku Klux Klan),
lawyers (like Judah P. Benjamin, with his reputation for
Levantine guile and his patina of mystery, as well as his
proximity to Jefferson Davis), and Indian chiefs (like Al Rosen,
from Spartanburg, South Carolina, the former Cleveland third
baseman who became the team's general manager).   The first Jew
to hold elective office in American history, perhaps even in the
modern world, was Francis Salvador, who served in the first and
second South Carolina provincial congresses before he was
scalped by Indians.   The first movie cowboy, the star of The
Great Train Robbery, and therefore the antecedent of Tom Mix and
Hopalong Cassidy and John Wayne, was "Bronco Billy," a falso for
Gilbert Anderson, né Max Aronson, born and raised in Little
Rock, Arkansas.   Even stranger was Marx E. Lazarus, a mystic, an
Abolitionist, a vegetarian, and a utopian who joined the
Alcotts' Brook Farm.   He was "probably the first Jewish
socialist in the history of the United States," according to
Lewis Feuer, though Lazarus later served as a Confederate Army
private before dying in obscurity.   Here surely is the stuff of
fiction, though perhaps not realistic fiction (since few readers
would believe it).   And yet Southern Jews remain in the missing
persons bureau of the republic of letters, although they belong
to a heritage that provoked Mordecai Richler's father -- a scrap

dealer -- to ask, when the Canadian's first novel was about to
be published: "Is it about Jews or about ordinary people?"[29]

But if any important writer of Southern Jewish background
has emerged, it is Lillian Hellman. She was born in New Orleans
in 1905, where her paternal grandparents had come during the
German immigration of the 1840's. Her mother, Julia Newhouse,
had been born in Demopolis, Alabama, to a family of bankers and
storekeepers. From the age of six until the age of sixteen, she
resided and attended public schools in both New York City and
New Orleans, where she did not stay. Beginning in the 1930's
came a series of theatrical successes, including The Children's
Hour (1934); Days to Come (1936); The Little Foxes (1939); Watch
on the Rhine (1941), which won the Drama Critics' Circle Award;
and Another Part of the Forest (1946). Hellman is undoubtedly
the most distinguished female playwright ever to live in America
-- though such praise may appear faint, upon reflection.

Although she is also the only literary figure of Jewish
birth canonized in the Encyclopedia of Southern History, her
career testifies to the elusiveness of such designations. She
cannot be convincingly categorized as a regionalist, nor as a
recorder of Jewish life there or elsewhere. In reviewing the
most informative study of Southern Jewry ever written, Eli
Evans' The Provincials (1973), Hellman doubted whether "there
ever was a 'South' even during the artificial confederation of
states to fight the Civil War." Similarly she asserted that
"Jews are as unalike as most other people, only, as somebody
else said, more so."[30] She is not beguiled by the
vicissitudes of either Southern or Jewish history, not does she
write directly about Jews.

When asked whether the rapacious Hubbards of The Little
Foxes and Another Part of the Forest were based on anyone she
had known, Hellman once cryptically replied: "Lots of people
thought it was my mother's family." Later, as her
autobiographical volumes were published, the mask was peeled
off. When she remembers hocking the ring that her uncle Jake
had given her for graduation and then reporting to him what she
had done, he replied: "So you've got the spirit after all.
Most of the rest of them are made of sugar water." The lines
reappear in The Little Foxes. Hellman admits to experiencing
greater difficulty with writing that play than any of her
others, because it "had a distant connection to my mother's
family and everything that I had heard or seen or imagined had
formed a giant tangled time-jungle in which I could find no

space to walk without tripping over old roots . . . " For she
herself had remembered the Sunday dinners with her mother's
family, "with high-spirited talk and laughter from the older
people of who did what to whom, what good nigger had consented
to thirty percent interest on his cotton crop and what bad
nigger had made a timid protest, what new white partner had been
outwitted, what benefits the year had brought from the Southern
business interests they had left behind for the Northern profits
they had sense enough to move toward." Given such ugliness it
is understandable that she underwent conflicts with her mother's
family that were not successfully resolved until The Little
Foxes was written.[31] The Hubbards, although they are given
names like Ben and Leo, do not in any way betray an ethnic
identity, which must have produced a purr of satisfaction from
the defense organizations fighting against bigotry.

Gratifying though such obfuscation may be, Hellman's
sensibility allowed little place for speculation upon the
mystery or history of the Jews. Members of her family were
quite assimilated and unaffected by their ethnic origins, and
seem to have exempted themselves from religious observance or
belief. Such indifference made them typical of many Southern --
and American -- Jews. Her immediate social world was Jewish, as
was her husband Arthur Kober, who was once admired for his comic
Jewish dialect tales. But Hellman herself has lacked explicit
interest in the Jewish people, with whose fate she has not
directly associated herself. Even after visiting the Maidanek
camp after the Red Army had liberated it, Hellman does not
bother to mention that the overwhelming majority of the victims
were Jews.[32]

She went to some length to evade confrontation with the
deeper recesses of Jewish history and destiny. Her appearance
before the House Committee on Un-American Activities resonated
with her gallant statement that she would refuse to cut her
conscience to fit that year's fashions. It has been less
noticed that she did not make the customary invocations to the
Judeo-Christian tradition, but instead announced that she
respected and had tried to abide by the "ideals of Christian
honor" alone. These included truthfulness and the refusal to
bear false witness (which, if memory serves, were first
promulgated on Mount Sinai), the prohibition "not to harm my
neighbor" (cf. Leviticus 19:18), and loyalty to her country
(which, despite all evidence to the contrary, she has not deemed
inconsistent with support for Alger Hiss).[33]

Scoundrel Time (1976) more fully reveals how poorly she fits into the category of Southern or even Jewish writer. The region has hardly been, for American radicalism, a burned-over district, and only a small fraction of American Jews have been radicals. Yet Hellman, without ever quite boarding the Dixie Special, still purchased a one-way ticket on that train to the Finland Station. For her memoir is far harsher on Americans who opposed Communism, often foolishly and crudely and spitefully, than it is on the Stalinist system that consigned nameless millions to their deaths in the Gulag Archipelago. Soviet terror claimed more lives than did the Holocaust. Yet Scoundrel Time prefers to criticize those who cooperated with the McCarthyites, such as "the children of timid immigrants," who, for all their admirable industriousness, intelligence and energy, "often . . . make it so good that they are determined to keep it at any cost."[34]

Hellman makes no attempt to demonstrate the validity of such a generalization, which is in fact quite unpersuasive. Eight of the "Unfriendly 10" were from such a background, as were other uncooperative witnesses like her fellow playwright, Arthur Miller. Among the most cooperative Hollywood witnesses, on the other hand, were Gary Cooper, Ronald Reagan and Robert Taylor. Nor does Hellman identify herself with the Jewish spirit of dissidence, which she might have praised, averring instead that "whatever is wrong with white Southerners -- redneck or better -- we were all brought up to believe we had a right to think as we pleased, go our own, possibly strange ways."[35] Such amazing disregard of the conformist pressures in Southern society -- on race, the Lost Cause, labor unions, radicalism, and atheism -- is downright bizarre, though it does reflect one way of resolving the possible tension between being Southern and being Jewish. Hellman's remarks indicate a certain pride in the region of her birth that she could not, or would not, summon for her Jewishness.

Other writers from the South have rarely treated Jewish life there or elsewhere, and have shown little effort to invent Jewish characters. In the canon of regional letters, there is no Robert Cohn or Meyer Wolfsheim or even Henry Bech, much less any characters conceived as indelibly as Fagin or Daniel Deronda or Leopold Bloom or Shylock or Monsieur Swann or Nathan the Wise. Mark Twain once blamed the Civil War, with its nimbus of romanticism, upon Sir Walter Scott; but no Southern novelist followed Scott's example of drawing upon Philadelphia's Rebecca

Gratz for the model of Ivanhoe's Rebecca. Demography alone cannot be held accountable. Jews have constituted a tiny fraction of the population of western and central Europe. And yet of the major authors in twentieth century fiction, one (Kafka) was Jewish, and another (Proust) was half-Jewish. Three others (Virginia Woolf, Thomas Mann, Vladimir Nabokov) were married to Jews. Not only does the most important novel of the century (Ulysses) make a Jewish character into Everyman, but Thomas Mann also located the Hebrews in modern literature in Joseph and His Brothers. Nor are other ethnics entirely absent from Southern literature, even though few Southern whites can trace their ancestry outside the British Isles and few are not Protestant. But figures like the Irish-born father of Scarlet O'Hara, or Stanley Kowalski, or the deaf mute Antonapoulos in The Heart is a Lonely Hunter are not easily forgotten.

The Jews who are mentioned in the literature of the region tend not to live there. Charleston's William Gilmore Simms set Pelayo (1838), a romance in which Jews are prominent, in eighth-century Spain.[36] In the fourth section of "The Bear" (1942), the Jew who has come to Yoknapatawpha is described as "solitary, without even the solidarity of the locusts and in this [there was] a sort of courage since he had come thinking not in terms of simple pillage but in terms of his great-grandchildren, seeking yet some place to establish them to endure even though forever alien." Here the Jew meets the moral standards Faulkner exalts above all others -- the capacity to endure through perpetuation of the family and through valor. But no individual Jews are named or identified. In The Sound and the Fury Jason Compson is, besides his other faults, a bigot. But his targets are distant and also abstract -- Eastern Jews. Individual Jews appear briefly in several of Faulkner's novels, however -- in Soldier's Pay (1926), Mosquitoes (1927), Sanctuary (1930), Pylon (1935), A Fable (1954), and others. Alfred Kutzik, the closest reader of these books to investigate the portrayals of such figures, has speculated that the unflattering portraits are due to Faulkner's willingness to make the Jew "a symbol of the rapacity and inhumanity of modern industrial society. This is why . . . the only bosses and traveling salesmen and shyster lawyers in his writngs are Jews."[37] But Jews are hardly prominent in Faulkner's fiction, which is characterized by a low estimate of the human estate itself, from which few are exempt.

The Southern writer who most often had the Jews on his mind
was Thomas Wolfe, an author who had difficulty sundering his own
attitudes from those of alter egos like Eugene Gant and George
Webber. This point is important because of the reputation for
anti-Semitism that continues to hover over Wolfe's work. His
agent, Elizabeth Nowell, claimed that he "had the villager's
dread and dislike of urban Jews." Louis Rubin had added, rather
defensively: "It was because there were Jews in the city, and
not because he naturally and primarily hated Jews as such, that
Wolfe wrote his so-called 'anti-Semitic' passages."[38] Wolfe's
first novel, set in the South, partly bears this out. The Jews
in Look Homeward, Angel, like the boarder in the Gant home or
the owner of the grocery store down the street, are depicted in
kindly, or at least not unsympathetic, terms. When Gant moves
north, in Of Time and the River, the meditations on the Jews
become more frequent; and some of the passages become unsavory.
Is it because Jews are metropolitan that they are described,
among the undergraduates Gant teaches in New York, as "all
laughing, shouting, screaming, thick with their hot and swarthy
body-smells, their strong female odors of rut and crotch and
arm-pit and cheap perfume, and their hard male smells that were
rancid, stale and sour"?[39]
     Nevertheless such depictions can easily be countered with
many others that are favorable and admiring; and whatever his
discomfort in the city may have been, the Jewish East Side is
made vivid as "the richest, most exciting, the most colorful
[part of] New York he had ever seen." Gant becomes a close
friend of one of his Jewish students, Abraham Jones, "a
wonderfully good, rare, and high person"; and Jewish women are
depicted as sexually desirable and enticing. In The Web and the
Rock, posthumously published, Gant has become Webber,
experiencing a tumultuous affair with Esther Jack, described as
half-German and half-Jewish. This relationship is presumably
modelled on Wolfe's own affair with the stage and costume
designer Aline Bernstein, whom Wolfe referred to as "my Jew."
Wolfe and his protagonists were certainly somewhat ambivalent
about Jews; the antagonism is always qualified and often
undercut by expressions of admiration and attraction. Perhaps
the strongest case against Wolfe's anti-Semitic reputation was
his response to Nazism. Though his novels were very popular in
Germany, he made clear before his death in 1938 his sympathies
with the Jewish victims of barbarism, which he considered "the
spiritual disease which was poisoning unto death a noble and
mighty people."[40]

The shadow of German racism extended to the South as well, and some Southern writers acknowledged its moral repugnance. Flannery O'Connor mentions the Holocaust in one of her letters, claiming that she was "always haunted by the boxcars." She added, quite aptly, that "they were actually the least of it."[41]   Katherine Anne Porter's only novel, Ship of Fools (1962), set on a German liner bound for Mexico in 1931, is not set in the South, but includes a Jewish character, a salesman of Catholic religious objects, who is already segregated from the "Aryan" passengers.

Two novels attempt to render more explicit some connection between the racial injustice that has scarred Southern history and the persecution that culminated in Nazi genocide. In Harper Lee's Pulitzer Prize-winning To Kill a Mockingbird (1960), it is current events time in the classroom of Miss Gates, who denounces the German government's undemocratic discrimination against the Jews, who "contribute to every society they live in, and most of all, they are a deeply religious people. Hitler's trying to do away with religion, so maybe he doesn't like them for that reason." Miss Gates cannot acknowledge that the Nazi motive might not be anti-religious but "racial"; and sensitive Scout Finch realizes, however inarticulately, that Miss Gates, like other respectable whites in the town of Maycomb, Alabama, is a hypocrite. Scout's father Atticus, an attorney and a man of honor, cannot even listen to Hitler on the radio, whom he dismisses as "a maniac." Only one set of Jews seem to be living in Maycomb, and the Levy family has been there for five generations. Atticus recalls that, around 1920, the local chapter of the Klan "paraded by Mr. Sam Levy's house one night, but Sam just stood on his porch and told 'em things had come to a pretty pass, he'd sold 'em the very sheets on their backs. Sam made 'em so ashamed of themselves they went away." If only sardonic wit and the power to shame with such effectiveness had been employed more often in actual towns like Maycomb. In any event Atticus acknowledged that the Levy family "met all the criteria for being Fine Folks."[42]   How vulnerable such families might have been to the canaille had they not met local standards of excellence, had they been "freethinkers," or had they tried to address black residents as social equals -- these possibilities were unstated.

Like Eugene Gant, Stingo in William Styron's Sophie's Choice (1979) has to go north from Virginia to find Jews and to brood on their qualities. True, his first love had been Miriam

Bookbinder, "the daughter of a local ship chandler, who even at the age of six wore in her lovely hooded eyes the vaguely disconsolate, largely inscrutable mystery of her race." Like Gant, Stingo claims to resemble "numerous Southerners of a certain background, learning and sensibility, [who] . . . have from the beginning responded warmly to Jews." (Styron's own wife is Jewish.) One of the three central characters, who live in a Brooklyn apartment, is a Polish Catholic survivor of Auschwitz, Sophie Zawistowska. The second is Nathan Landau, supposedly a brilliant but crazed, Harvard-educated scientist. He is a nasty figure upon whom Styron grants the honor of a distinctively drawn and compelling personality. Stingo himself is depicted as haunted by the history of slavery, a topic he will treat in fictional form later by focusing on the Nat Turner rebellion.[43] (Any resemblance to any living persons is surely not coincidental.) Styron himself is nothing if not ambitious and, unlike Katherine Anne Porter, treats the death camp experience itself, rather than the antecedent period. And he does so not allegorically but directly. His victim/survivor is Gentile rather than Jewish, and Styron/Stingo has to get out of the South to confront the anguish of Jewish history. But it is a rare, though not reckless, attempt by a Southern novelist to do so.

Like Stingo, Will Barrett in Walker Percy's latest novel, The Second Coming (1980), remembers an early crush. This time its object is Ethel Rosenblum, a cheerleader who beats out Will as the class valedictorian. "She was short, her hair was kinky, her face a bit pocked," he recalls. "But as if to make up for these defects, nature had endowed her with such beauty and grace of body, a dark satinity of skin, a sweet firm curve and compaction of limb as not easily to be believed." As the novel opens however, Barrett is experiencing a middle-age crisis, requiring the attention of a physician. For among the symptoms is his impression that Jews could no longer be found in that part of North Carolina. "Weren't there Jews here earlier?" he asks Dr. Vance, who replies: "Well, there was Dr. Weiss and Dutch Mandelbaum in high school who played tackle." And the doctor concedes that those two men are no longer around, though the novel itself notes that the ten thousand Jews in North Carolina, with their twenty-five synagogues and their median family income of $21,000, constitute a "small, though flourishing" community. Yet Will Barrett is disturbed because the absence of Jews represents a sign of some sort: "When the

Jews pull out, the Gentiles begin to act like the crazy Jutes and Celts and Angles and redneck Saxons they are. They go back to the woods." The non-Jews, he fears, were "growing nuttier by the hour."[44] Here is an unanticipated task assigned to the Chosen People -- to save the sanity of the goyim (as though obedience to 613 divine injunctions were not burdensome enough). But in its own way, The Second Coming is a representative Southern depiction of the role of the Jews, who are noteworthy for their absence.

The South itself has rarely been treated in the fiction of American Jews either. It is as though, like certain other parcels of real estate in the past, this particular territory were restricted, for Gentiles only. Perhaps only one well-known novel by an American Jew, A Walk on the Wild Side (1956), is set in the region. But Nelson Algren, né Abraham, was only partly Jewish; and his depiction of the underside of New Orleans (called "N'wawlins") hardly counts as local color. It is not animated by an interest in the special characteristics of the city or its environment. Set on Perdido Street, the tale is, according to Algren himself, "really about any street of any big town in the country," as the following passage suggests: "In the cheery old summer of '31, New Orleans offered almost unlimited opportunities to ambitious young men of neat appearance willing to begin at the bottom and work their way up the ladder of success rung by rung. Those with better sense began at the top and worked their way down, that route being faster."[45] Other books might be mentioned. Perhaps the central character of The Naked and the Dead (1948) is Sergeant Sam Croft, but he comes from west Texas; and the novel itself is set primarily on a mythical island in the Pacific. Mailer himself has tried to be many things in his life, from white Negro to Aquarius to mayor to President, though the one identity which he has tried to elude is "the nice Jewish boy from Brooklyn." But ever since the film version of All the King's Men, he writes, he has "wanted to come on in public as a Southern demagogue" -- surely one of the most bizarre ambitions to which any novelist has ever admitted. An electronics salesman from the Bronx achieves the White House that eluded both Mailer and Willie Stark in Michael Halberstam's The Wanting of Levine (1978). Like our first Chief Executive, Alfred Levine has made a considerable fortune in his real estate investments. He also displays considerable skill getting along with "crazy backwoods farmers in the South," which is part of his territory, and in bedding compliant, lonely Southern women. The wisdom and compassion that Levine exudes not only make him welcome in the region, despite his cosmopolitan literalism, but also make Halberstam's tzaddik with a sample case a most appealing American President.[46]

The Southern whites in The Wanting of Levine are not only libidinous but decent and amiable and fair-minded; but this benign portrait must also be set against the fears of bigotry which the region has tended to inspire. By now such fears can be twisted for humorous purposes, as in The Great American Novel (1973), in which Philip Roth imagines a baseball team owned by a Jewish family named Ellis (after the Island). A rookie -- a young man from the provinces -- is shocked by this discovery, writing home as follows: "Dear Paw we bin trickt. The owner here is a ju. He lives over the skorbord in rite so he can keep his i on the busnez. To look at him cud make you cry like it did me just from lookin. A reel Nu York ju like you heer about down home. it just aint rite Paw . . . "[47] In such passages Roth manages to mock Jewish anxieties about anti-Semitism as well as the benighted prejudices of kids like "Slugger." Roth's only rival as a national resource of humor, Woody Allen, had a nightclub routine in which he visits the South and is invited to what he believes is a costume party. The others in the car taking him to the party are all wearing sheets. One of the passengers, who is referred to as a "grand dragon," seems to be their leader, Allen conjectures, because he is wearing contour sheets. Then Allen realizes what is occurring. His own identity is revealed when, instead of donating money to the cause, he makes a pledge. As he is about to be lynched, his whole life passes in front of him: the swimmin' hole, the country sto' where he has gone to fetch some gingham fo' Emmy Lou, and fryin' a mess o' catfish. Then in an ultimate sign of the schlemiel, Allen realizes that "it's not my life" but someone else's, thus deriving laughter from the recognition of the incompatibility of being both Southern and Jewish. Incidentally the routine has a happy ending: Allen makes a brief speech in behalf of brotherhood, and the inspired Klansmen give money to Israel Bonds.[48]

Such routines suggest the possibility that the Jew and the Southerner, who have confronted one another so infrequently and so obscurely in the pages of serious fiction, have met with greater resonance in popular culture. There, if anywhere, gospel singers have encountered jazz singers. Roth's imaginary

letter points to the possibility of finding Jews in folklore and
legend whom Southerners might have preserved in oral
traditions. And the contributions of Jews to media-made Dixie
also require investigation. Such a study might include Jerome
Kern and Oscar Hammerstein's musical Showboat (whose interracial
theme can be found in other Broadway productions that Jews have
written), David O. Selznick's masterpiece of the primal screen
Gone With the Wind (partly written by Ben Hecht), the Gershwins'
Porgy and Bess (which Oscar Levant once called "a folk opera --
a Jewish folk opera"), and even Al Capp's Dogpatch. Sid Caesar
once parodied Southern speech on Your Show of Shows, describing
his insomnia: "I'm having more trouble sleepin' than a
gray-eyed possum fleein' from the hungry, saliva-filled jaws of
bayin' hounds in the black swamp on a foggy night in the middle
of the month of July." In a Mike Nichols-Elaine May routine, a
playwright named Alabama Gross concocts a tale whose heroine has
"taken to drink, dope, prostitution -- and puttin' on airs."
Tom Lehrer satirized the region in "I Wanna Go Back to Dixie"
(1954), describing decadence, pellagra, the boll weevil,
lynchings, and cornpone. There "ol' times . . . are not
forgotten, whuppin' slaves and selling' cotton."[49]

    The influence of such images has undoubtedly been far more
extensive -- and perhaps more intriguing -- than in American
Jewish fiction, which has found little space on Mr. Sammler's
planet for the region that has so enthralled the imaginations of
others. But that is another story.

ARTSCROLL: AN OVERVIEW

B. Barry Levy
McGill University

Begun in 1976 as a 136 page English commentary on Esther,
the Artscroll Bible commentaries have flourished in a way few
observers would have thought possible. The series has now
passed the 20 volume mark, and while publication has decelerated
of late, the project continues to grow.[1] In the course of its
rapid rise in popularity, Artscroll has managed to attract the
support of many spokesmen of different Orthodox groups. Few
other efforts -- educational, religious, political or literary
-- are able to display letters of approval from Rabbis M.
Feinstein, M. Gifter, J. Kamenecki, G. Schorr, J. Ruderman, A.
Zlotowitz, S. Kotler, and D. Cohen and also official endorsement
from The Union of Orthodox Jewish Congregations, strong support
from in-house publications of the Montreal Vaad HaIr and the
Council of Young Israel, and accolades from The Jewish
Observer. The editorial board of Tradition has shown
inconsistency in its attitudes by publishing a critique of
Artscroll and then, in effect, retracting it by supporting a
counter criticism by one of its editors, but Tradition remains
the only Orthodox journal to have published any serious
reservation about the project.[2] These official endorsements
have helped the series' popularity. The volumes are frequently
spotted in the hands of synagogue-goers and students; they have
become standard acquisitions in synagogue libraries. Frequently
given as gifts, they even sneak into the occasional college
library or lecture. Why?

The Artscroll volumes seek to full a perceived void in the
traditional literature on the Bible that is available to the
English reading world. Most available commentaries, it would
seem to the editors, suffer from being scientific, apologetic,
critical and/or untrustworthy. These faults extend to the
translations on which they are based and derive from the
exegetical attitudes they express. They are not even
authentically Jewish, it is claimed, as they often rely upon the
contributions of non-Jewish writers. One of Artscroll's goals
is to replace these unacceptable commentaries. Though never
mentioned by name, the apparent objects of disapproval are the

commentary on the Torah edited by Rabbi J. H. Hertz and the
similar commentaries on the rest of the Bible edited under the
direction of the Rev. Dr. A. Cohen, both published by the
Soncino Press.

The foremost English contribution to Jewish Bible study of
the earlier part of this century, Hertz's work began to appear
in 1929, has been reissued in various one-volume formats, and
may be found by the dozens and hundreds in virtually all North
American synagogues. Its popularity is best attested by the
number of copies published, but its impact has, to the best of
my knowledge, never been evaluated. Using the British and
Foreign Bible Society's Hebrew text and the Jewish Publication
Society's 1919 translation as a base, Hertz produced a highly
eclectic commentary on the Torah including the observations of
the Jewish and non-Jewish ancient, medieval and modern writers
listed on pages 976-979. Hertz's policy of "Accept the truth
from whatever source it comes" (Maimonides, Introduction to
Shemonah Peraqim) is stated at the outset and attempted
throughout the work. One might criticize his penchant for
excising and including the favorable comments of writers hostile
to his religious outlook, for this creates a false sense of
scholarly and critical approval. Nevertheless, Hertz succeeded
in presenting a commentary which for several generations has
served as a popular model of the mixture of religious tradition
and modern scholarship.

Since there is no other work worthy of the attention that
also fits the criticisms of the Artscroll editors, I must
conclude that Artscroll has as one of its raisons d'être the
refutation of almost every aspect of the Hertz and Cohen
efforts. Hertz and Cohen used the Jewish Publication Society's
translation; Artscroll produces its own. Hertz and Cohen used
both Jewish and non-Jewish writers, Artscroll only approved
Jewish ones (except for occasional lapses into the likes of
Josephus Flavius and Yefet ben Ali).[3] Hertz and Cohen
identified their sources; Artscroll provides biographical
sketches as well. Hertz and Cohen covered the entire Bible;
Artscroll is doing likewise and (like Hertz) has extended its
interests to liturgical texts, but is working on the Mishnah and
other things as well. Hertz and Cohen used only English in the
commentary; Artscroll translates almost everything, but includes
much Hebrew material also. Hertz and Cohen initially produced
eighteen rather small volumes (the Torah was later republished
in different formats); the Artscroll project is likely to fill

50-75 volumes. Hertz and Cohen tried to be true to the tradition and sensitive to modern scholarly issues; Artscroll has disavowed any involvement in the latter. Hertz and Cohen addressed the English speaking world at large; Artscroll is concerned with a smaller but more committed reading public.

The vast differences in both physical and ideological makeup, as well as the number of copies in print and their relative costs, mean that the replacement of the Hertz-Cohen volumes will be slow and incomplete. Barring a change in format, Artscroll will not attain the popularity of Hertz as a companion to the weekly Torah reading. As a text for study, though, particularly for the hundreds of less known and untranslated traditional works, it is a useful source of material and may very well help to stimulate a renewed interest in the entire field of traditional Biblical interpretation. But, as I have clearly demonstrated elsewhere, the effort has been marred by serious shortcomings that call the entire project into question.[4]

Directed at early teenage day-school students, Hebrew teachers, college students, housewives, uninitiated adult readers, kollel scholars, and yeshiva students, Artscroll must be perceived as a major work, intended for a wide readership that includes many people who are at home with Bible study and can appreciate the comments included. As obvious as it may seem, this point is important, for it means that the volumes must withstand the test of sophistication as well as readability, reliability and accuracy. In spite of the editors' repeated appeals that the volumes are not the final word, must not be used for halachic decisions, and should, if properly used, lead to further study of the original sources, the extent of the effort, the size of the projected series, the range of the audience addressed, the project's initial success, and the extent to which the books are used in Jewish schools, lead me to believe that the editors are consciously working to produce the official, authoritative, English Bible commentary for religious Jews, one that will remain for generations the base of Bible study for all but the few who have the ability, time and inclination to probe further into the original sources.

Every Artscroll volume contains the Hebrew Bible text, a "new" English translation, and extensive comments on each verse. The commentary, undoubtedly the most important part of the effort, attempts to collect and organize relevant interpretations from a host of acceptable Jewish writers.

Supplemented by introductions to individual units (books, chapters or weekly lections) these commentaries have become the repository of what most readers assume to be the correct "orthodox" interpretation of the Biblical text. In fact, there is no such thing, and herein lies one of the series' central flaws.

While ancient (pre-Mishnaic) Jewish writings have the Bible as their major focus, this concern is shared by only a portion of the post-Mishnaic literature. As the Talmud grew in importance, it and non-Biblical concerns dominated religious writings. Later the Zohar also refocused attention, as did philosophical and halachic works in all periods. To be sure, the Bible remained a major concern, but it was usually read in the light of these other texts, and many (if not most) works that interpreted the Bible in the last 2000 years have been more concerned with using the Bible as a basis for transmitting independently determined non-Biblical notions than presenting those of the Bible itself. In the process, rabbinic tradition dominated the field and actually surpassed the Prophets and Hagiographa in practical importance, religious authority, and the number, size and quality of the books whose production it stimulated. Much of this situation was recognized over the centuries and opposed in various degrees by rabbinic and non-rabbinic writers who fought to give scripture an independent hearing. Ibn Janach, Ibn Ezra, David Kimchi, the Rashbam and others frequently contributed to this approach to the texts, but their commitments to medieval rabbanism limited the extent to which they could break completely with tradition. Karaite writers were somewhat freer in this respect, but philosophical and polemical needs often colored their interpretations no less than non-Karaitic ones. Other writers challenged specific issues or assumptions about Biblical interpretation, but their impacts are often felt more in their attitudes toward earlier interpreters or commentaries than in the articulation of their assumptions or the establishment of hermeneutical rules or procedures. However one evaluates the individual contributions of these writers, the heterogeneous nature of the field is immediately apparent to any serious reader. Commentators worked with different sources and used different assumptions, and their commentaries differed accordingly. These authors frequently approached their very personal task with reverence and awe, as aware of the responsibility as of the difficulty in interpreting God's words or messages. While many of them attempted to

outline some of the principles used in their work, most failed
to produce detailed rules of procedure. Such rule books were
written to guide students of the Talmud, and a vast (though
frequently neglected) literature evolved, but this field touched
only tangentially on the Bible. The lack of a formal
hermeneutical literature coupled with a diffused interest in the
Bible itself has left Jewish writers without a field of
hermeneutical study comparable to the Christian one.[5]

Possessing a very rich interpretative literature on the
Bible but lacking an official Orthodox program that suggests how
to use it, Artscroll has worked on its own. While no real
hermeneutical statements have been published, and it is not
clear that any exist, we can reconstruct some of the procedures
from the methods used in the many volumes in print.[6] The
comparison of these principles with the classical rabbinic
commentaries allows us to see how Artscroll fits into the
history of Jewish interpretation of the Bible. The wide based
support for the series gives a clear picture of how the
contemporary Orthodox rabbinate understands the Bible and wants
it taught to the present and future generations of Jewish
readers.

Artscroll's Hidden Agenda

Some interpreters of the Bible are readily observable as
rationalists; others, as mystics. Hasidim, Mitnagdim,
midrashists, scientists, grammarians, preachers and others
contributed to the literature of Biblical interpretation. Each
of these groups (and their individual representatives) went
about the business of interpreting the Bible in different ways,
and they often disagreed about how to proceed in general as well
as about the meanings of specific passages. In fact, one of the
most pervasive but frequently ignored stimuli for most of the
traditional commentaries on the Bible was dissatisfaction with
the available commentaries.[7] While to some extent this type
of bold discontent was voiced more with respect to recent
writers or contemporaries than those of the more distant past,
in many cases centuries, not decades, separated critic and
subject. The existence of these strong reactions to the earlier
exegetical efforts is to be expected, for if the writers did not
feel that the Bible said something to them that had not yet been
said by everyone else, they would have no justification for the
composition of yet another commentary on the holy text. And
while these earlier traditionalists felt a deep reverence for

the efforts of their teachers and predecessors, they also felt
able to improve upon them and to offer differing opinions within
certain limits (though these limits varied with the different
writers). More significantly, they stated these feelings openly
and consciously involved the readers in both the exegetical
processes and the arguments in order to win them over to their
points of view. Artscroll, in contrast, frequently voices its
rejection of certain exegetical ideas but expresses overt
dissatisfaction only with those outside the rabbinic tradition
as Artscroll perceives it. Secular humanists, scientists,
irreligious Jews and Christians may be wrong in their statements
or approaches or attitudes. Dissatisfaction with the views of
the rabbis and their statements is never voiced, and the freedom
of expression felt and exercised by the earlier writers seems to
be lacking.

Covert dissatisfaction is another matter. Many of
Artscroll's rabbinic predecessors were committed to the
intellectual developments of their times, and these writers
articulated many ideas that Artscroll finds hard to accept.
Where questions on the use of science, the need to ignore (or at
least not rely upon) many midrashim, the role of God in human
history, the nature of Biblical miracles, and the correct way to
determine what actually happened in ancient times (to mention a
few) were resolved by early authorities in ways contrary to
those deemed proper by Artscroll, statements reflecting these
attitudes have been omitted. Other passages that fit
Artscroll's fundamentalist agenda are included from these same
writers. Also, many important individuals were omitted from
consideration, giving the impression that Orthodox leaders like
Rabbis A. Kook and J. B. Soloveitchik, as well as the famous
Orthodox Bible expert Nehama Leibowitz, are unworthy of
inclusion. Omission of Italians like S. D. Luzzatto, U.
Cassutto and the 16th century writer Azariah de Rossi is also
significant and helps us to appreciate the limitations imposed
on the process of selection.

Certain issues are also avoided or minimized.
Notwithstanding the statements of the baraita cited in the
Babylonian Talmud, Baba Bathra 14b, beginning with the
discussion of the Gemarah, a.l., there has never been complete
agreement on the authorship of all parts of all of the books
assigned in the baraita. According to Ibn Ezra twelve (not
eight) verses at the end of Deuteronomy were added to the Torah;
Abarbanel disagreed with the dating and authorship of several

books in the introduction to his commentary on Former Prophets;
the attribution of Proverbs, particularly the last two chapters,
to Solomon, has received less than unanimous support; various
sources have added Ezra to the talmudic list of contributors to
Psalms; the question of the authorship of Job was never settled;
the beginning and end of Ecclesiastes have been attributed to
the editor, not the author, etc. Some of these books have not
yet been commented on by Artscroll, but the problem of
authorship is a pervasive one. However one views the give and
take of the question, it must be conceded that there is much
more discussion than one might deduce from the meager attention
given to the issue and the simplistic manner in which it is
discussed.[8]

Similarly, concern for the literary qualities of the Bible
was an integral part of the analysis of some earlier writers.
Repetitions in wording or content received a great amount of
attention as did the occurences of leitwoerter and visible
patterns of literary expression (for example as developed in the
various cycles of events in the story of the plagues in
Exodus). Nachmanides in particular was very interested in the
literary qualities of the Torah, and some of his comments have
found their way into the Artscroll volumes. Modern literary
analysis of Biblical narratives is a natural development of this
field, is far from the hostile criticism it is assumed to be,
and adds an important dimension to one's understanding of the
text. Literary sensitivity necessitates careful study of every
text as a unit and stresses the dynamics of the whole as well as
the significance of individual parts. The integration of such
an approach, definitely in keeping with the attitudes of some
traditional commentators, would offer an important balance to
many of Artscroll's observations that tend to remove individual
units from their literary contexts and, in the process, allow
them to assume meanings of only 'secondary and tertiary
importance without ever explaining their primary significance.
Unfortunately, such comments are rare.

Another traditional literary concern that is only minimally
reflected in Artscroll is an awareness of the qualities of
Biblical poetry. After the observation that Biblical poetry is
composed in Hebrew, the next most obvious observation is that it
is composed of balanced lines, a phenomenon usually referred to
as parallelism. The existence of parallelism is not a modern
discovery, as may be seen from the discussion of this phenomenon
in the writings of Menachem Ibn Saruq, Rashi, Rashbam, Ibn Ezra,

Radak, etc.,[9] and the Artscroll translations have taken note
of this structural pattern by printing the translation of poetic
passages in poetic form. A corollary of the parallel nature of
Biblical poetry is that it is repetitive, or, to be more
precise, in expressing any given idea, it is stylistically
appropriate to repeat the idea in parallel lines. This, too,
was known by the medieval authors, though they did not always
agree on the exact nature of this double expression, or on when
it represented two versions of the same thought and when it was
to be taken as different innuendos, not exactly identical.

Both positions were espoused on various occasions and often
discussed. Though obviously familiar with some of these
passages, the Malbim frequently rejected as out of hand the
possibility that there could be any sort of repetition in the
Bible and that one might properly assume, like the earlier
masters, that any two lines actually say the same thing. This
approach necessitated a careful analysis of the Hebrew lexicon
and has enriched our understanding of Hebrew synonyms. But it
might have been tempered with the observation of the earlier
writers that there is such a phenomenon as "repetition of the
same idea in different words." While the Artscroll volumes
occasionally discuss the problem as it relates to individual
passages, this issue, important as it once was and still is,
does not receive the attention it deserves. This gives the
impression that the only valid approach to Biblical poetry is
that of the Malbim, who categorically denied the possibility of
such a literary form.[10] Interestingly, the lack of complete
commentaries by the Malbim and Hirsch (who also engaged in such
linguistic endeavors) on Lamentations has visibly altered this
aspect of the Artscroll presentation of that book.

Anyone versed in Jewish Biblical interpretation will thus
observe that Artscroll has taken the step of choosing those
rabbinic exegetical procedures it finds most appropriate and
rejecting those it opposes, but unlike many of its predecessors
it has not explained the criteria for selection or openly
discussed and refuted the positions it rejected. The reader is
led through a selection of explanations and told what the texts
mean. He is not involved in the processes of interpretation, is
not expected to understand how the interpretations were derived,
and is not encouraged to choose the approach that suits him
best. Surely few readers can appreciate the extent to which
this process has colored the presentation of the Bible they have
received.

Like precious pearls that have been stimulated by some irritant in the oyster, so are many of the _midrashim_ and traditional exegetical comments stimulated by (real or apparent) ambiguities, questions, grammatical difficulties, or contradictions. It is these problems or questions that have engaged all who would explain the text and have, to a large extent, shaped their understanding of it. Of course there are other factors, and all writers did not address themselves to all of the problems, nor did they necessarily agree on what the problems were, but it is the _problems_, the irritants if you will, that lie behind the interpretative literature, and these problems must be presented, defined, and solved.

The definition of the problem before its solution has not always been part of the classical commentaries. Indeed one of the main concerns in the study of Rashi has always been defining the problems that gave rise to his comments. Nonetheless, there are models like the commentaries of Abarbanel and Rabbi Isaac Caro where the problems are clearly defined, and this must be the pattern of any anthology that would compare the comments of various writers on the same phrase or word. This procedure would give definiton to the verse and would clearly focus on the issues in the Bible text while allowing free expression of general matters developed by individual writers. Such an open system, focusing on the questions and the suggested answers, would also convey the impression that other possible answers may exist and would stimulate new ideas as much as it taught the content and appreciation of the old. It would make the give and take, the arguments, and the analysis the main concern. Focusing on the answers without the problems turns discussion and analysis into fiat and a system that encourages thoughtful creativity into dogmatic antiquarianism.

Virtually all Bible commentaries and _midrashim_ have been stimulated by one stimulus -- the Bible text -- and a collection of comments from these works that fails to make this the primary focus gives the impression that the words of the sages are of primary importance, not the scriptural passages on which they commented. Appropriate descriptions of the volumes that seemed to be sensitive to this question are those of Rabbi Moses Feinstein, who originally saw the Artscroll production as anthologies of "precious things" collated from the words of the sages. In his early approbations he failed to state that these volumes are actually commentaries or explanations of the Bible, but this has been altered in Volume 6 of Genesis.[11]

On the surface, Artscroll appears to be an anthologized commentary containing excerpts from and paraphrases of traditional writings on the Bible, but this is only partly correct. The sources on which it is based have been reworked, edited, misrepresented and systematically censored to present its own new image of the Bible.[12] It may fancy itself the voice of the past, the presentation of a "Chazal's eye-view" of the Bible, but only some of the sources are old, while the attitudes imposed on them are late twentieth century East - Euromerican Yeshiva World. One might question how such a revolutionary development has been promoted by writers whse entire effort is allegedly designed to be so conservative, but such are the strengths of Artscroll's unhistorical approach.

We may conclude that the editors are radical innovators without even being aware of it. But it is also possible that through selection of certain models and controlled censorship of others they are consciously working to redirect the way in which traditional Jews understand the Bible.

On Modernity in Bible Study

The past few centuries have witnessed many varied trends in the study of the Bible, but "modern" Bible study is distinguished by several factors. Starting with Spinoza and those with him who form the beginnings of Biblical criticism, we see a growing challenge to the divine authority of the Bible, a serious doubt about God's role in the Bible's formation, and distrust of the Bible's claim to relate what really happened in antiquity. While this skeptical attitude has become the basis of much that passes for modern Biblical scholarship, it is not the primary characteristic of being "modern". Beginning with the discovery of the ancient Near East by Napoleon, learned readers of the Bible have reoriented their approach to the holy text in a conscious effort to see the Biblical characters in the light of their authentic ancient environments rather than as reconstructed in the clothes, habits and ideologies of the ages of the readers themselves.[13]

To be sure, no amount of archaeological data from cognate civilizations will enable the absolutely certain recovery of the ancient past, and even the availability of original documents directly related to the events in the Bible will not answer all of the possible questions.[14] But this type of approach, stressing the ancient, original context of the Bible rather than its current homiletical potential, is what distinguishes modern

Biblical study from that of centuries and millenia ago. Approaches that dispute Spinoza's philosophical skepticism would be called religious, as would those that insist on the relevance of the Bible for modern life. Those that totally ignore the study of antiquities are simply not modern. Traditional Jews may feel somewhat threatened by this notion, because rabbinic tradition has based its claim on a vertical pattern of authentic transmission from antiquity to the present, and some pious readers may feel uncomfortable in a horizontal approach that stresses only ancient sources and preferably those close in time and space to the text under discussion. But surely there can be no serious threat to religious belief from the ancient artifacts, texts and buildings that were used by the very people about whom believers so strongly desire to study.[15] To be sure, there is a wide gap between the attitudes of many of the modern scholars who make these materials available to the general public and the religious leaders who ignore them; but it would seem crucial that this material not be ignored and that it be subjected instead to the same rigorous analysis to which the traditional commentators submitted the non-traditional sources available to them. Only in this way can the useful aspects of the data be made available to strengthen the commitment of the faithful on scientifically verifiable grounds wherever possible.

Of course the comparison of these ancient materials (usually documents) with the related parts of the Bible will not necessarily confirm all aspects of the traditional interpretations of the Bible. Their challenges to the authority and accuracy of the Bible are as much a function of the nature of the authority and accuracy assumed to exist as the testimony of the Bible itself, and they do offer possible solutions to exegetical questions that have been answered differently by the commentators over the centuries. Thus the challenge is primarily directed at the commentators, the midrashim, and the philosophers, and, it requires reexamination of the approved writers of previous generations, a process that was routine over the centuries but has gone out of style in certain latter day Orthodox circles. Religious readers need not reject all that has gone before; a serious reading of these materials more than justifies a careful study of many of the treasured commentators right along with the best of the modern writers (and some contemporary critics have come around to this way of thinking).[16] But the process of Biblical interpretation is an ongoing (perhaps never ending) open search. Religious Jews should rely on the classical, medieval, and modern traditionalists for contributions in the areas of their strengths, but, they might also seek out, examine and assimilate the relevant elements of the scientific contribution of modern times, for avoiding this last step violates a principle hallowed by centuries of earlier Jewish writers. This procedure has not been followed by Artscroll, which avoids all contact with these discoveries.

Modern study also stresses the importance of historical perspective, an attitude accepted by Artscroll. Thus in Eichah, (p. xxxv) the reader is asked "Can someone pretend to understand today's Sephardic Jews without understanding nineteenth century Yemen and Morocco? Or understand Ashkenazi Jews without knowing the Pale of Settlement and Austro-Hungarian Empire?" While the subjects are obviously more complex than these questions might suggest, any exhaustive analysis must include these concerns. Following Artscroll's formulation, I feel compelled to ask two similar questions. "Can someone pretend to understand the Jews of the Bible without understanding ancient Canaan and Mesopotamia? Or can one understand the Israelites who wandered in the desert without understanding the world of ancient Egypt and the Pharaohs?" The unfortunate fact is that virtually all historical perspectives on the ancient, medieval and modern books cited and discussed in the volumes are lacking. The reader is never given any serious historical information that can be used to evaluate the contributions of anyone cited. What point is served by these grand questions? The Artscroll effort has fallen short of its own standards.

Another point of interest in modern Biblical studies, especially important because of the development of literary criticisms of various types, centers in the names of God that appear in the Bible, particularly in the Torah. Frequently modern scholars lose sight of the fact that areas which concern them have bothered intelligent readers of the Bible before, and that alternate solutions have been offered; in this case, the Artscroll selections should go far to dispel this misconception. Throughout the volumes we frequently find careful attention given to the various divine names, including an ongoing attempt to understand exactly what may be deduced from certain unexpected or apparently inconsistent usages. It is difficult to determine if the editors' interest in this subject comes from the desire to collect random earlier comments or to refute one of the essential elements of modern criticism;

there is no hint either at the challenge or at any of the
solutions that modern scholars have offered. In any case, the
authorities excerpted in the commentaries, particularly the
medieval ones, were definitely sensitive to the problem, and in
the Artscroll volumes we find a good but disorganized sample of
the older responses that have been proposed.[17]

There are other aspects to modern Bible study, but these
typify Bible study only as part of the general field of modern
inquiry. Thus, for instance, no modern scholar would consider
studying any ancient or medieval text from a popular edition, if
a critical one were available. The thousands of variant
readings and citations from published manuscripts and early
writers are invaluable in reconstructing the best possible
versions of the Mishnah, targumim, talmudim, midrashim and
medieval writers, and, again, there are important and extensive
efforts along these lines by Artscroll's religious precursors.
This is another religiously acceptable form of research that
Artscroll has avoided, and by so doing the editors have not only
repudiated one of the most useful sources of precise information
on dozens of important texts; they have also popularized,
perhaps even sanctified, vulgar editions, inaccurate readings,
and errors, all in the desire to be uncritical and
unscientific.[18]

Torah and Scientia

One of Artscroll's major concerns is the avoidance of
influence from unapproved sources of interpretation. Not
content with simply anthologizing the many traditional
commentaries, Artscroll has evidenced open hostility to all that
it does not accept as valid. This means that this other
material has been considered and rejected.

Occasional references to non-traditional sources point to a
strange inconsistency that must be pressed, but the implications
of this criticism of general knowledge lead to an important
observation. While most (but not all) of the time the Artscroll
series accurately presents the words of the authorities and
sources it cites, through its refusal to utilize materials
beyond those canonized by these sources and to apply these
sources to contemporary issues it has failed to provide
traditional answers for the questions and intellectual
challenges facing the modern reader. The Artscroll response to
the huge number of linguistic, historical and archaeological
discoveries of the past century is to declare them scientific

distortions or, more frequently, to omit them entirely and to insinuate that others who do not similarly bury their heads in the sand are apostates of a sort.

To be sure, there is a vast Jewish exegetical literature that ignores scientific inquiry and intellectualism, but there is also a huge corpus that does not. Criticism of Artscroll's narrowness may be derived from careful study of the same religious writers on whom its editors drew and not from some external, heretical ideology or even from the Jewish writers they omitted. Briefly, Maimonides routinely analyzed the pagan literature for its bearing on understanding the Torah and even made it the basis of his rationale for the mitzvot; Nachmanides cited the Apocrypha and an archaeological discovery of his time; Abarbanel constantly made use of the interpretations and observations of non-Jewish writers; most of the medieval philosophers produced works that are syntheses of traditional Jewish sources and various combinations of Aristotelian and neo-Platonic philosophies. Menasseh ben Israel's Conciliator (cited in Bereishis, p. 528) is an excellent example of this type of blend of Jewish and non-Jewish sources in a commentary; Rabbi Z. H. Chajes cited and explained the importance of many ancient texts from the Apocrypha and elsewhere; Rabbi David Hoffman also utilized these materials constantly in his exegetical writings.[19] The list could be longer, but the point is clear. Facts were used from all sources. Artscroll has not accepted this principle. To be fair, it should be noted that a small amount of scientific information is found in Artscroll, but it is rarely quoted firsthand. Thus Aaron Marcus, the author of Kesset HaSofer, was able to utilize some archaeological data that he found relevant, and Artscroll may quote it even if it does not correspond with information made available from other traditional sources, but no contemporary archaeologists or their works are ever mentioned. The maps in Yehoshua, for example, are based on the work of Rabbi J. Schwarz, who died in 1865. Certain geographical information is provided to complement the statements of the approved writers, and astronomy is referred to on occasion, but there is really very little pure science included in the books and virtually nothing of the other scholarly disciplines that have been developed and that might have made important contributions.

The problem of the admission of scientific data into Orthodox thought has been dealt with at some length by Russell Jay Hendel.[20] He begins by citing passages from the Talmud,

Maimonides, and elsewhere that openly state that knowledge,
including what one might call the physical sciences, is Torah.
He then "intuitively" rejects this idea in favor of a definition
of Torah that relates to the source of a statement, not its
content. This logic, when applied to Bible study, yelds the
observation:

> Rabbis are often confronted with anti-traditional
> statements coming from Biblical criticism.
> Intuitively, one would like to classify these
> statements as heretical. Yet, this seems inconsistent
> with acceptance or recognition of apparently similar
> statements among some Rishonim, who made statements
> differing from the accepted Talmudic opinion.
>
> This dilemma vanishes as soon as we realize that, like
> Talmud Torah, epikorsus (heresy) is defined by its
> source, -- not just by its content. The Rishon's
> antitraditional statement, [sic] emanates from an
> ideologically committed person who is attempting to
> study our tradition by logically analyzing Biblical
> texts. The epikorus' antitraditional statement [sic]
> emanates from an antiideologically committed person
> analyzing Biblical texts. Thus, the Rishon, on both a
> personal and textual level, relates to a source of
> kedusha -- hence, his act is one of Talmud Torah. The
> epikorus, however, relates on a personal level to a
> source of Toomah (uncleanness) and epikorsus -- hence
> his act is classified differently.[21]

Nothing could be clearer. Only the author of a particular idea
is important; the content of the idea is all but irrelevant. It
is very difficult to correlate this notion with the attitudes of
the medieval writers under discussion, but Hendel's statement
undoubtedly reflects the thinking of many contemporary Orthodox
Jews and, in the absence of any formal statement, appears to be
a close approximation of the Artscroll position.

All else aside, the system breaks down when it comes to
dealing with errors in the scientific data, an aspect of the
problem that Hendel has ignored. As man's knowledge of the
world has advanced, many of the scientific claims of earlier
epochs have been refuted or replaced by later ones. Thus some
of the scientific observations that were incorporated into the
authoritative religious literature of earlier centuries need to
be brought in line with certain modern perceptions, but their
inclusion in these works has given them canonical status, and
one is therefore faced with the need to modify their status
because of scientific advances. This is perceived as
desecration of sacred texts.

The presence of this outside material in the writings of
approved authors must mean that its admission was not

prohibited, and some writers insist that it is even necessary.
A worthy model for enterprises like Artscroll is Maimonides'
methodological note in the introduction to his commentary on
Pirqei Avot (Shemonah Peraqim), which he saw as a collection of
other writers' observations:

"Know that the ideas that I will present in these
chapters and in the subsequent commentary are not of my
own invention, nor are they explanations that I
discovered, but rather I have gleaned them from [a] the
words of the sages in the Midrashim, in the Talmud, and
in others of their works, also from [b] the words of
the philosophers, both ancient and recent and also from
[c] the works of many [other] people -- Accept the
truth from whoever said it."

Priority was given to the words of the sages, but the teachings
of ancient and (for Maimonides) modern philosophers were also
included, as were the relevant and correct ideas of many other
people. Truth was not the monopoly of philosophy, or of
antiquity, or even of rabbinic authority. It was accepted from
wherever it came; its source neither precluded nor guaranteed
its being truth, and the directive to accept it (Arabic:
'sm^c, imperative) is unmistakable.[22]

Artscroll's procedure has failed to carry out this program.
The reader is blocked from using the most advanced knowledge
available, but he is told that he cannot deal with the halachic
problems of megillah readings on Purim that relate to questions
of walled cities (The Megillah, pp. 125-6); that a woman who
resigns herself to widowhood for ten years to the day loses the
ability to bear children (Ruth, p. 75); that the purpose of
leaves on plants is to protect the fruit (Tehillim, p. 62); that
chiromancy is meaningful (ibid., p. 225); that an increase of
light would enable people to see very small objects (Bereishis,
p. 40); that the gestation period for a snake is seven years
(ibid., p. 128); that man was originally created a duparsophon
(double body, male and female) (ibid., p. 167); that the stars
can influence human destiny (ibid., pp. 510-511;[23] etc., etc.
These statements cannot be considered reliable, in as much as
they ignore the potential contribution of scientific exploration
(e.g. dating walled cities) and include folklore in place of
scientific fact (e.g. the gestation period of snakes).

One of the most interesting examples of the misapplication
of ancient science centers on the kidneys. In several places
Artscroll notes that the kidneys are the seat of the intellect
(Bereishis, p. 409, Tehillim, p. 622, etc., based on Rosh
HaShanah 26a, etc.). This notion is then utilized to explain

how Abraham managed to observe the Torah before it was given to Moses -- his "spiritual kidneys" filtered out the waste of the world and left him with Torah purity. To be sure the basis of this comment is rabbinic (Gen. Rab. 61:1) and Rabbi Gifter, who apparently is the source of the spiritual kidney theory, may have intended it metaphorically. But how can a modern reader be expected to accept either the rabbi's claim about kidneys or the assumption underlying the application of the claim to Abraham's observance of the mitzvot?

All of these observations are quoted from authoritative writers; the reader is expected to believe them. The editors have anticipated to some degree that some Orthodox readers may not accept all of these unscientific statements, for in some places where the literal meanings of rabbinic statements contradict what science has proved to be true, the texts are explained metaphorically. The effect is to hold that because earlier writers tried to explain the Bible in the light of the science of their days, contemporary Orthodox readers are bound, if not literally then in some metaphoric way, by their errors, and they must accept ideas that were not at all what the original writers intended. It would be valuable if future Artscroll writers consider more carefully the words of the Taz (Divrei David, Gen 2:23): "We should not divest the words of our rabbis of their simple meanings."

The value of using scientific determination in religious matters has been strongly supported by Rabbi M. D. Tendler in his reply to Rabbi A. Soloveitchik's criticism of his position on the halachic status of brain death:

> "The interface of ethics or religion and medical practice is a treacherous area because it demands dual expertise to traverse it safely. In the issue at hand, a mastery of the fundamentals of physiology is necessary for the proper elucidation of the talmudic references."[24]

Clearly Tendler believes that the correct understanding of the passage, in this case based on the ability to differentiate between the two possible meanings of a text, may be had only with the benefit of scientific training. A similar dual expertise must be demanded in Biblical interpretation and in the reading of secondary sources that would explain the Bible, but under most circumstances textual interpretation is part of the Humanities, not the Sciences, and this is a much more touchy business.

Torah (Orthodox teachings) and Science, originally thought
to be incompatible, have become united by limiting Science to
technology and leaving speculation, interpretation or value
judgments to Torah.[25] This united front of the two supposedly
invincible disciplines, Torah and Science, now confronts the
Humanities as subjective, ephemeral, human distortion. Anyone
who attempts a response to a particular problem using the
methods or values of the Humanities is, by Artscroll's
definition, operating outside the Orthodox camp; in Artscroll's
words he is "a secular humanist." What is so seriously missed
in this position is the realization that religious thought as it
developed over the centuries, also included what we would now
designate as aspects of the Humanities, though the fields of
late seem to have parted company. The conflict of Torah and
Science against the Humanities is thus the result of Science's
generally acknowledged resistance to this sphere of thought and
Orthodoxy's facile rejection of it for being anti-Torah and not
even scientific. Actually Torah and the Humanities have much in
common (perhaps a source of the tension between them) and much
to learn from each other. They would profit greatly from a
closer relationship, even if Science were to become a little
jealous.

Above I described an Orthodox attitude towards Science that
values but limits scientific elucidation. Such an attitude is
typical of the publications of the Association of Orthodox
Jewish Scientists, where one sees highly educated, even
decorated scientists blending (what appear to be) sophisticated
scientific arguments with religious thought. Totally lacking in
many of their presentations is a comparative level of
sophistication in treating the Judaic elements of their work.
The blend is incongruous, but obviously works for many educated
people. Orthodox thinkers might consider adding to the proposed
treatment of a given problem the perspectives available from
other intellectual disciplines. The opportunity to employ the
Humanities could afford the insights of history, linguistics,
geography, comparative literature, philosophy, etc., all of
which have counterparts in the extant religious literature. The
challenges presented by these and other academic disciplines may
also prove valuable and stimulate new attempts at Orthodox
interpretation of the Bible.[26] Should this happen, the
advantage of hindsight would be present, in that previous
attempts at religious appropriations of the academic disciplines
would be available for scrutiny. The penalty for intellectual

failure would be greater, though, as would be the criticism of "borrowing," which is almost inevitable in some areas.

It hardly needs to be stated that neither of the positions just outlined has been followed by Artscroll. The Humanities are shunned and Science is basically ignored, leaving Torah to be studied by itself, as if that were really possible. The doctrine that the only proper sources to be used in the elucidation of the Torah are Torah-sources is clearly enunciated in Rabbi Gifter's Hebrew forward to Bereishis I. This brief document deserves to be translated into English for those readers who are unable to read the Hebrew, but for now I must excerpt several statements. Most interesting is the principle that "God's Torah may be explained only in the light of Torah." This idea dovetails with the Rabbi's statements that the Oral Torah embodies the only proper explanations of the written Torah, that no non-Jewish efforts to understand the Torah are acceptable, and that any deviation from the Oral Torah in the explanation of the Written Torah is heresy, even in the narrative portions that contain no obvious references to halachic practice. This elimination of all options in the analysis of Biblical narrative and poetry (even non-halachic passages) is very radical, particularly when compared with the many traditional commentators who did not accept this position, but what is most striking is its similatiry to the teachings of a 17th century philosopher who, in his desire to free Biblical interpretation from the clutches of subjective rabbinic distortion, stated "Our knowledge of scripture must then be looked for in scripture only."[27]

The difference between the attitudes of Rabbi Gifter and Spinoza is at the same time very great and very slight. Spinoza limited scripture to scripture, while for Rabbi Gifter scripture is "Torah" in general, but both men limit the terms of reference to the closed corpus under discussion. Spinoza, of course, added certain claims for the ability to use reason as a tool of exegesis; Rabbi Gifter has not addressed himself to this particular question. It is difficult to know the extent to which he is prepared to trust human reason, but he presumably does so not at all when it comes into conflict with anything considered Torah. The fact that he has declared any deviation from the Oral Torah to be heresy may not be surprising, but some attempt should have been made to correlate this position with those of the earlier, more flexible rabbinic authorites. I suggest that Spinoza did not emphasize the value of archaeology because he lived before the advent of the archaeological age and did not fathom the role that modern discovery might take in illucidating the Bible.[28]   Rabbi Gifter, while he would appropriately reject Spiniza's religious skepticism, also has no use for discoveries.   His approach therefore lacks both of the characteristics of modernity, and we must conclude that while Spinoza's position is partly modern, Rabbi Gifter's is premodern! Given the sanctity attributed to Jewish tradition and the general hostility of the modern world to religion, it should be obvious that nothing insulting is intended by this observation.   But, if this attitude really reflects a premodern unawareness of recent discoveries and the ability of these discoveries to advance the cause of true, accurate, Torah-, Orthodox (or whatever term one may wish to use to describe) Bible study, can it really serve to convince, much less to guide, twentieth century people?   One who accepts this approach is fenced in from both sides.   On the one hand, he is unable to deviate from anything handed down in the tradition; on the other hand, he is barred from taking seriously anything else that may seem of value in treating a problem.   If ever there was a doctrine that justified Toynbee's claim that Judaism is a fossil, this is it.

The "Torah Version of History"

A Passage in The Megillah (p. xx) states: "Most of us have become indoctrinated with a non-Jewish, anti-Torah version of history."   It is hardly worth debating how the writer knows this, but one might justifiably assume that Artscroll believes itself to be the correct, Torah-version of history.   No formal definition is presented, though, and we must deduce for ourselves exactly what is meant.

Artscroll works on the assumption that all narratives in Torah-sources report events that actually occurred.   This is not the place to enter into the debate on allegorical interpretation of the Bible or the difference of opinion between Maimonides and Nachmanides on the historicity of many of the narratives in the Torah, but one must note that the approved literature does allow for the possibility that some of these stories are not historical events.[29]   This also seems to be the principle underlying the following passage from the Zohar:

Rabbi Simeon said, "Woe to the person who says that the Torah's purpose is simply to teach stories and the words of commoners. For if that were the case, even today we could produce a Torah from the words of commoners, even better than the others . . . Rather all the words of the Torah are the real matters and lofty secrets . . . '" (Vol. III, 152a). Similarly, rabbinic literature is replete with discussions about the historical value of many Talmudic and midrashic passages. Responses to unbelievable stories ranged from dogmatic acceptance to forceful rejection. A middle position called for reinterpretation of the passages, thereby avoiding both the problems and the need to reject the texts. Obviously some traditional writers realized that the purpose of rabbinic midrashim need not be the presentation of an accurate description of past events; others disagreed. If these writings were not intended to be historical, then it is inappropriate to treat them as such on the assumption that it would be unfaithful to do otherwise. It may not have been easy, but traditional commentators over the years have worked with midrashic literature as a form of Biblical exegesis that demonstrates great sensitivity to the text, preserves essential aspects of ancient law and lore, and contains important sources of religious teachings, without assuming that all of it is historical.[30]

The implications of such an approach are extremely pervasive and require re-evaluation of popularly accepted views of such matters as: patriarchal observance of the mitzvot and rabbinic legislation; the doctrine that the Torah existed before the creation of the world; the accuracy of the rabbinic images of Biblical figures; the claim that the entire Torah (the Pentateuchal text) was given to Moses on Mt. Sinai; the letter-perfect accuracy of the Biblical text, including the Torah; and the assumption that all Biblical (or even talmudic and post-talmudic) books reflect one unified approach on any and all subjects. Some traditional writers were committed to the more controversial (and now unorthodox) positions on these and similar issues; they are not new, critical, or scientific corruptions that have no place in authentic religious literature. Lengthy lists of sources on these and many other similar problems may be culled from the same approved writers whose teachings fill the Artscroll pages. Selective disregard of these problems by Orthodox writers has placed many people in the position of not recognizing what is a traditional religious posture and what is not. Serious treatment of these issues as an ongoing part of Orthodox intellectual interests can only

serve to strengthen the commitment of the uncommitted, one of
the avowed purposes of the Artscroll effort.

To a large extent the problems of reconstructing Biblical
history depend on the careful reading of many narrative
passages, and these are the texts that have been subjected to
the most midrashic manipulation. Thus, if one is to probe
Biblical history, he must first peel off the layers of midrashic
analysis and get down to the bare text. Artscroll need not
reject all midrashim, but it should focus on their purposes.
Some midrashim were composed to teach moral lessons, others for
halachic reasons; some represent important theological and
philosophical statements, others were intended as jokes. The
assignments to categories are sure to meet with less than
unanimous support, but the attempt should be made. Of course
the real conflict arises when a midrash appears to have been
written with historical intentions but really is not accurate.
Nonetheless, the general attitude of many early writers was
flexible, and one need only turn to the statements of Hai Gaon,
Ibn Ezra, Maimonides, Nachmanides and many others to see that
acceptance or rejection was very subjective. Note, for example,
the words of Shemuel HaNaggid:

> "You should know that everything the sages of blessed
> memory established as halachah in matter of mitzvah,
> which is from Moses Our Teacher, peace unto him, which
> he received from God, one should not add to it or
> detract from it. But what they explained with regard
> to Biblical verses, each did according to what occurred
> to him and what he thought. We learn those of these
> explanations that make sense, but we don't rely on the
> rest . . . "31

This feeling is not limited to medieval authorities, or to
Sephardic intellectuals, as may be seen, for example, from the
writings of the nineteenth century figure Rabbi Zvi Hirsch
Chajes.32   In contrast, a non-judgmental attitude toward
midrash is reflected in various contemporary writers. Thus, the
Hazon Ish: "And I return to the simple belief in the Oral Torah
and I don't engage in arguing 'why'; my only desire is to be
like a simple Jew who relates 'what' he received."33   And
Rabbi Ahron Kotler: "No part of Torah [halachah, aggadah, dinim
and stories (his words)] can be properly assessed by man using
only his limited faculties."34   This highly midrashic posture
is not new. It dominated Biblical interpretation in ancient
times and exerted a tremendous influence in some medieval
circles, but the early midrashic approach was replaced,
suppressed and/or manipulated by many medieval writers, so that
they could use the midrashic material they wanted and bypass the

rest. With the rise of the mystical influence, particularly
strong in the sixteenth to eighteenth centuries, rationalism was
replaced by another midrashic approach that frequently absorbed
and strengthened the early attitudes that had been circumvented
previously.[35] Following this period, the Jewish community
lost its more unified attitude on this matter, and different
groups favored approaches that could be called mystical,
talmudic, scientific, midrashic and rational as well as various
mixtures of them. Each group, in turn, claimed authoritative
sources for its approach, and, because of vacillations that had
occurred over the centuries, each really could justify itself
within the overall traditional Jewish world. Further external
stimuli such as the Enlightenment, the development of Reform
Judaism, and the advance of scientific discovery also helped
shape the various Orthodox hermeneutics, all drawing from a
common pool of writers, but each contributing its own elements
and producing a literature different from the others.

Whether motivated by the rejection of Reform, acceptance of
certain mystical teachings (particularly when supported by
earlier rabbinic doctrine), the generally perplexed nature of
belief in today's world, or some combination of these and other
factors, Artscroll has followed a model of interpretation that
accepts midrash as historical. While many midrashic passages
could, in theory, be discussed as part of the traditional,
multi-layered exegesis, and occasionally they actually are, the
impression given the reader is that the primary level of
interpretation is, in fact, the midrashic one.

Traditional Jewish hermeneutics offer a commentator the
choice to accept or not accept midrash as history. Since the
Artscroll approach sees midrash as primarily historical, and
since it presents this view as correct and binding, a serious
conflict is generated with other sources of historical
information that contradict certain midrashic statements. If
the midrashim must be taken as presented, then the faithful must
believe: that David knew of Homer (Tehillim, p. 251); that the
King of Nineveh at the time of Jonah was the Pharaoh of the
exodus (Yonah, p. 124); that because no wars were mentioned
before Genesis 14, there were, in fact, none (Bereishis, p.
473); that Abraham, Joshua, David and Mordechai were the only
men whose coinage was accepted throughout the world (ibid., p.
429); that Ishmael married women named Adisha and Fatima (ibid.,
pp. 767-8); etc. Artscroll's presentation of late Biblical
history also follows rabbinic teachings and dates the

destruction of the first Temple in 423 B.C.E., the building of
the second Temple in 353 B.C.E., etc.

Various precedents would have allowed Artscroll to avoid
literal acceptance of midrash had it wanted to do so, but the
contemporary Orthodox world is highly receptive to unhistorical
approaches and uncritical thinking. That it prefers believing
in lore of the ancients -- who were unhistorical and uncritical
-- to confronting modern issues is somewhat understandable. But
its rejection of those classical writers who already fought
these battles means that contemporary Orthodoxy, to the extent
it supports Artscroll, is very much a product of the mystical
and folklorist mindset that was revived in the sixteenth to
eighteenth centuries under Kabbalistic influence after having
been seriously weakened by the medieval rationalists (whose
piety and acceptability, ironically enough, the contemporary
Orthodox world continues to acknowledge, at least in theory).

Many of the Artscroll volumes have their sitz im leben in
pious liturgical contexts rather than literary, historical or
text-analytical ones. The fact that the Torah, Psalms and the
megillot were chosen to inaugurate the project is also
significant. Unlike the Israeli, scholarly-traditional series
of commentaries Da^{c}at Miqra', which has yet to publish a
volume on the Torah, Artscroll has accepted this challenge
almost from the outset. Strong precedents for interpreting the
Torah are of great help in this endeavour, but perhaps another
dimension of exegetical and ideological influence is being
expressed. In describing mystical interpretation of the Bible,
Scholem observes: "A large part of the enormous Kabbalistic
literature consists of commentaries on Books of the Bible,
especially the Pentateuch, the Five Scrolls, the Psalms, the
Song of Songs, the Book of Ruth, and Ecclesiastes."[36] The
list is redundant, but with the exception of Jonah, which was
published for use on Yom Kippur, the first Artscroll volumes in
print correspond to those in Scholem's list. One might see the
similarity as coincidence -- liturgical interest being the
factor that motivated the Kabbalistic writers also -- but
another possiblity presents itself, namely that Artscroll shares
this same interest in mystical matters or at least receives a
significant stimulus from the twentieth century residue of this
earlier mystical activity. The choice of Daniel and Ezekiel
(also of mystical importance) to follow in the series bears this
out, as do Artscroll's Zoharic attitude on Biblical history and
frequent references to Hasidic ethics and philosophy. The ready

acceptance of the Artscroll enterprise by the contemporary
Orthodox world may be seen as evidence for the fact that such
mystical values or notions have survived and/or been revived in
this American Jewish community. Whether this is true for other
aspects of Jewish life is worthy of study; a positive response
is very possible. I believe this influence is unquestionably a
factor in the way this group of Jews studies, teaches, and
preaches about the Bible.

Conclusion

Lack of space prevents an exhaustive comparison of
Artscroll's procedures with those of its rabbinic predecessors,
but a number of points are clear. There are traditional writers
who favored the use of non-Jewish or non-traditional sources in
Biblical interpretation and others who opposed the idea.
Artscroll has followed the latter. Some traditional writers did
open battle with their rabbinic predecessors; Artscroll imitates
those who prefer to ignore the traditionalists they reject, but
it openly rejects non-traditionalists. Rabbinic writers were
divided on the use of science, on the obligation to follow
midrashic exegesis, on the rationalization of Biblical miracles,
and on the need to accept the narratives in religious sources as
historical. In each case Artscroll has sided with the less
rational, more naively faithful groups.

Many writers stressed how the problems in the Bible text
stimulated their responses. Artscroll imitates those who did
not, preferring to present the disputed results of serious
enquiries as fact. It has ignored most of the literary
considerations of the earlier writers in favor of midrashic
analysis. It gives lip service to historical perspective but
eschews any serious use of it. It prefers vulgar editions of
religious texts to critical ones and gives the impression of
being totally uninvolved in contemporary intellectual or
scholarly matters, even though there are rabbinic predecessors
acceptable within Orthodoxy who encouraged both.

Many of these attitudes are probably accepted by most
contemporary Orthodox Jewry. The interplay of European,
Israeli, American, scientific, Zionist, religious, secularist,
reformist and nationalist elements in today's Jewish world is
fascinating to observe but potentially dangerous to certain
religious interests, and the Artscroll positon on this interplay
is clear and strong, though I expect that not all equally
committed readers will be able to identify with the fears it

seems to express. There are some very positive modern contributions to the understanding of the Bible, and the acknowledgment of these contributions can only enhance several millenia of serious Biblical interpretation and simultaneously add to the credibility of one's rejection of those other elements of modernity that really are useless or even hostile.

In searching rabbinic literature for a school of exegesis that parallels Artscroll or served as its model, we may rule out some groups immediately. The philosophical works of Maimonides and his followers may be dropped from consideration, as may the Spanish exegetes (e.g. Ibn Ezra, Abarbanel), the massoretes, the North-African philologists (e.g. Ibn Janach) and the modern religious intellectuals (e.g. Rabbis Z. H. Chajes, David Hoffman, A. Kook). The French school of Rashi and the Tosafists is somewhat closer, but the peshat tendencies of Rashbam and Bechor Shor are far from Artscroll's real focus. Hasidic writers have had a strong impact on the work, as have other glossators (in contrast to commentators) of the past few centuries. Talmudic and midrashic teachings are felt throughout, but as interpreted through these same limited perspectives.

Ironically, almost all of these writers are cited, some quite frequently, but their impacts have been felt only slightly. In fact very few of the real influences on Artscroll's attitudes come from the classical Jewish Bible commentators. Most derive from homileticists, midrashists, glossators and others who used the Bible as the medium for spreading their religious teachings but were less than engaged by its literary qualities, problems related to its historicity, or other open intellectual concerns traditionally associated with Bible study. Rabbi Ahron Kotler's pamphlet How to Teach Torah is a good example of an American antecedent to Artscroll, though it, too, has roots in certain East-European circles of thought.

Except for its inconsistent usage of certain non-traditional sources and its huge number of factual mistakes, Artscroll's legitimacy as an expression of certain forms of Jewish interpretation is certain. It remains to examine why this particular presentation of the Bible has received such support from so many segments of the Orthodox community. A major factor in this acceptance is appearance. A quick look at the volumes will more than justify the unwary purchaser's expense. The books are attractively laid out, nicely printed, well bound, and aesthetically jacketed. They definitely look good. In addition, most of the volumes proudly display letters from highly respected yeshiva leaders. While the letters contain little evidence of actual contact with the books, the impression they create is one of strong endorsement. Should anyone look further, the layout -- with tables of contents, bibliographies and footnotes -- will give the impression of carefully documented research.[37] Why should anyone question their value?

A second reason the books have received such acceptance is their similarity to the kinds of exposure to the Bible Orthodox Jews receive. Synagogues and yeshivot rarely teach Biblical books seriatim. The Torah is often studied weekly, but most in-depth treatment of its contents comes in classes where the primary focus is the Talmud or in brief homiletical presentations. And many parts of the Bible are all but unknown. Serious study of the classical commentators is rarely pursued, and people generally prefer a homiletical bonmot to serious grappling with the text. Artscroll thus appeals to many minimally educated readers as a continuation of the superficial exposure to the Bible they receive in yeshivot and synagogues and may actually raise their levels of knowledge and awareness of certain texts and issues. But the series is not aimed at only the unlettered, and a number of writers have bemoaned the use of Artscroll as a school text, for without proper attention to original works in Hebrew, the next generation of Orthodox Jews may grow up unable to read the very books that served as the basis of Artscroll's collection.[38]

This is, I believe, very far from the intentions of the Artscroll editors, who constantly encourage the return to the rabbinic sources they used. A loss of ability to study Talmud, midrash and other rabbinic writings would be saddening to them and defeat one of their purposes. It would also leave the next generation of readers limited to studying Artscroll (and translations of the classics currently in progress). This would create a one-dimensional, homiletical approach to the Bible and prevent people from being seriously involved in the issues of Biblical study. Students and adults would be limited in their abilities to handle the originals. They would miss the dialectics, the problems, and the discussions and be forced to accept (or reject) only the teachings presented.

As far as this may be from Artscroll's intention, the project may well contribute to this eventuality. American Orthodoxy's increasingly monochromatic image is frequently

criticized.   The community is being pressed closer and closer
together.   Homogeneity of practice and -- more significantly --
of thought are being forced upon the Orthodox world as never
before.   Independent halachic decisions are becoming less common
as major problems are resolved through consultation with fewer
authorities, while Orthodox schools and synagogues seem to
orient their teachings and through them their followers to an
ever narrowing spectrum of ideas.   It was once fashionable to
discuss whether traditional Judaism should be called orthodoxy
or orthopraxy; the former term is now more appropriate.   While
commitment to observance is increasing in some circles (and
decreasing in others), doctrine has become more important than
it was, in some circles more important than observance; indeed,
observance without total acceptance of the contemporary version
of the rabbinic myth is considered inadequate, and Artscroll's
presentation of answers without questions and debate reinforces
the impression that this is correct.

Perhaps this myth was always important, but if so, its
acceptable form has changed in recent years, and the hybrid of
traditional religiosity and guarded intellectualism fostered by
moderate Orthodox leaders and institutions several decades ago
has given way to an Orthodoxy that is more insulated, less
intellectual and more extreme in its teachings.   Its models of
piety are more Hasidic, less philosophically sophisticated and
less tolerant of heterodoxy than those of earlier years.   It is
talmudically and midrashically oriented -- with all the positive
connotations this carries -- but it is also not really concerned
with the Bible.

This dominance of Orthodox education by rabbinic studies is
normal and to be expected, but the cumulative impact of years of
dealing almost exclusively with rabbinic texts and the lack of
concentrated, serious Bible study have taken their toll.   The
number of factual (not ideological) errors in the Artscroll
project is overwhelming.   Perfection is hardly a prerequisite
for publication, but the kinds of errors point to a serious lack
of high quality work in the area of traditional Bible study.
The rabbis who work on the project are working hard, but they
appear to lack the formal, disciplined training required for the
job; so do some rabbis who correct, edit and support the
project. The Orthodox community has thus come full cycle in
creating, supporting and perpetuating its own form of Biblical
interpretation, and it looks like it will be quite a while
before this orientation changes.   Those who are trained to do

the job lie outside Artscroll's Orthodox world, and there seems
to be little desire to master the academic fields of Biblical
studies, Jewish philosophy, history, and Semitic languages and
literatures, or to trust people who have done so and who take
these things seriously.

This situation also helps explain why the Orthodox
leadership has backed a project that claims to present only
traditional teachings, ostensibly adding nothing new on its
own. American Orthodoxy, like its traditional predecessors of
the sixteenth to eighteenth centuries, finds itself unable to
confront the contemporary intellectual issues inherent in Bible
study. Rapid changes in scholarly positions, a constant secular
pressure to erode commitment to traditional values and beliefs,
and an almost debilitating fear of modern ideas are all forcing
a return to classical sources and even a distrust of these
sources when they sound too modern. There were centuries when
writing supercommentaries on Rashi and Ibn Ezra took precedence
over explication of the Bible, partly because the attitudes and
techniques needed for proper Biblical studies were perceived as
foreign and hostile, and possibly because critical thinking
pushed the results of Biblical interpretation beyond the limits
deemed acceptable by the religious community. Whatever the
reason, we again find an observant community similarly limited
in its scope and circling back on its traditional sources, not
moving ahead.

While Artscroll's attitudes obviously reflect the needs and
aspirations of many Orthodox Jews, other forms of religious
expression stand in marked contrast to them, most notably the
Da^{c}at Miqra' series of Bible commentaries being published by
Mossad HaRav Kook. This Israeli press -- under Orthodox
direction, to be sure -- has to its credit an important (but
unfinished) series on the Bible that tries to present the best
of tradition and scholarship together. Apparently some forms of
Israeli Orthodoxy (perhaps because of Sephardic influence) are
more interested than their (Ashkenazi) American counterparts in
the values, not only the interpretations, of their more
intellectually open predecessors.

Perhaps this more sheltered North American stance may help
prevent assimilation -- intellectual if not social -- (or at
least it gives this impression), but it is not clear for how
long. Nor can I estimate the cost. One thing does seem
certain. Only when the pendulum swings back and the system
again opens up to the intellectual world -- showing the riches

of its heritage and exploring those of others -- will American
Orthodox Biblical interpretation be redirected towards its more
intellectual rabbinic predecessors.

NOTES TO "LOVE, MARRIAGE"

Biale

Research for this project was undertaken initially in 1980-81 in Jerusalem with the support of the Lady Davis Foundation and the American Council of Learned Societies. I wish to thank my colleagues, John Chaffee, Elizabeth Fox-Genovese and Gerald Kadish and my wife, Rachel Biale, for critical comments on the manuscript.

[1]Moses Mendelssohn, Gesammelte Schriften Jubiläumsausgabe (Berlin, 1929-1938), v. 16, 15 May 1761, letter 103, p. 205 and 27 April 1762, letter 200, p. 324. See further, Alexander Altmann, Moses Mendelssohn (University of Alabama, 1973), pp. 92-100.

[2]Jacob Katz, "Marriage and Marital Relations at the End of the Middle Ages," (Hebrew), Zion, 10 (1945-46): 47-49.

[3]See Michael Anderson, Approaches to the History of the Western Family (London, 1980), pp. 39-64.

[4]Edward Shorter, The Making of the Modern Family (New York, 1975) and Lawrence Stone, The Family, Sex and Marriage in England 1500-1800 (New York, 1977). A similar argument about the modernization of attitudes toward childhood was made by Phillipe Ariès in Centuries of Childhood, trans. by Robert Baldick (New York, 1962).

[5]See in particular the review of Stone's book by E. P. Thompson in New Society (September 8, 1977): 500ff. and Alan MacFarlane in History and Theory 28 (1979): 106-17.

[6]Andrejs Plakans and Joel Halpern, "An Historical Perspective on Eighteenth Century Jewish Family Households in Eastern Europe," in Paul Ritterband (ed.), Modern Jewish Fertility (Leiden, 1981), pp. 18-32. On the question of household structure in different parts of Europe, see Peter Laslett and R. Wall (eds.), Household and Family in Past Time, (Cambridge, 1972). On Eastern Europe, see Andrejs Plakans, "Peasant Farmsteads and Households in The Baltic Littoral, 1797," Comparative Studies in Society and History 17 (1975): 2-35.

[7]Azriel Shochat, Im Hilufei Tekufot (Jerusalem, 1960), pp. 162-73.

[8]Jacob Katz, Out of the Ghetto (Cambridge, Mass., 1973), pp. 34-35.

[9]See Sefer Hasidim, ed. Reuben Margaliot (Jerusalem, 1957), p. 334. See also pp. 370-1. H. H. Ben Sasson speculates that the explicit use of the word "love" (ahavah) in this text was influenced by the medieval doctrine of courtly love. See his History of the Jewish People (Cambridge, Mass., 1976), p. 553. In his review of Jacob Katz's Tradition and Crisis, Ben Sasson also argued, using other evidence than that presented here, that love was part of the norms of the Ashkenazic Jews. See Tarbitz, 29 (1960): 297-312 and Katz's rejoinder in Ibid. 30 (1961): 62-72. Ben Sasson's examples, as Katz noted, are quite peculiar and subject to other interpretations but together with the present argument suggest that Katz was too hasty in arguing that love was a private experience devoid of normative sanction.

[10]Abraham Ber Gottlober, Zikhronot u-Masa'ot, ed. R. Goldberg (Jerusalem, 1976), pp. 85-87.

[11]Solomon Maimon, Autobiography, ed. Moses Hadas (New York, 1967), pp. 20-21.

[12]Jacob Emden, Megilat Sefer, ed. David Kahana (Warsaw, 1897), p. 58.

[13]See David Roskies, "Ayzik-Meyer Dik and the Rise of Yiddish Popular Literature," (unpublished doctoral dissertation, Brandeis University, 1975), 48-101.

[14]Ayn Sheyne Historye fun aynem Mekhtikn Rovs Tokhter fun Konstantinopl un fun ayn Rov Zayn Zun fun Brisk (n.p., n.d.); see Roskies, 67-68.

[15]Genesis Rabba, 68; Leviticus Rabba, 8; Numbers Rabba, 2. See also the introduction to Tanhuma ha-Katan. On the theme of predestination in the chapbook literature, see Roskies, 68-70.

[16]M. Vishnitzer (trans), The Memoirs of Ber of Bolechow (London, 1922), p. 79.

[17]Stone, 605-7; H. R. Styles, Bundling: Its Origins, Progress and Decline in America (Albany, 1871); J. L. Flandrin, Les Amours Paysannes (Paris, 1975) and Idem., "Repression and Change in the Sexual Life of Young People in Medieval and Early Modern Times," Journal of Family History, 2:3 (1977): 196-210.

[18]Isaiah Horowitz, Sefer Shnei Luhot ha-Berit (New York, 1946), p. 100. Emphasis added.

[19]Ezekiel Landau, Noda Be-Yehudah, 2nd ed. (Prague, 1811), Q. 27.

[20]Moses Isserles, Responsa, edited by Asher Ziv (Jerusalem, 1971), Q. 30, p. 170.

[21]Texts of such legislation are collected in A. H. Freiman, Seder Kiddushin ve-Nisuin (Jerusalem, 1964), pp. 210-16.

[22]Yair Haim Bachrach, Havat Yair (Frankfurt, 1699), Q. 60. For a much less sympathetic attitude toward a similar case, see Jacob Reischer, Shvut Ya'akov (Halle, 1710, Offenbach, 1719, Metz, 1789), Part 2, Q. 112.

[23]See J. Hajnal, "European Marriage Patterns in Perspective," in D. V. Glass and D. E. C. Eversley (eds.), Population in History (Chicago, 1965) and Peter Laslett, The World We Have Lost (2nd ed., New York, 1971), pp. 84-112. See statistical data in Plakans and Halpern for Latvia in the eighteenth century.

[24]On the elite, see Gottlober, vol. 1, p. 85. That Jews married early was the common opinion in the Polish enlightenment. See Jacob Goldberg, "Jewish Marriages in Old Poland in the Public Opinion of the Enlightenment Period," (Hebrew), Galed, 4-5 (1975): 25-33.

[25]Pinkas Medinat Lita, ed. Dubnow (Berlin, 1925), para. 128, p. 32.

[26]Landau, 2nd. ed. Q. 54, p. 63 and Jacob Emden, She'elat Yavetz (Altona, 1738-59), Q. 14, p. 18. These two responsa contain general statements about the prevalence of child marriage in Eastern Europe, but virtually all of the responsa literature from the eighteenth century contains specific cases. Whether or not the practice was more common than earlier, it seemed to have constituted a more serious legal issue with authorities in both Germany and the East taking steps to curb it. On the legal history of child marriage, see Otzar ha-Poskim (Even ha-Ezer), Section 1, ch. 3, section 15.

[27]Landau, Q. 52.

[28]The Memoirs of Glückel of Hameln, trans. by Marvin Lowenthal (New York, 1977), pp. 23ff.

[29]The responsum was by R. Meshulam, the court president of Pressburg, in Moses Teitelbaum, He'shiv Moshe (Lemberg, 1866), end of book.

[30]Shivhei ha-Besht (Jerusalem, 1969), pp. 81-84.

[31]R. Isaac Meir Alter of Gur, She'elot ve-Tshuvot ha-Rim, (Biozepocz, 1867); Even ha-Ezer, Q. 26 (a case from Warsaw in 1850); Menachem Mendel Schneerson, Sefer Tzemach Tzedek (Brooklyn, 1945); Even ha-Ezer, Part I, Q. 34.

[32]Shivhei ha-Besht, 81-84 and tale # 249. The latter was omitted from the second edition of the Baal Shem stories and can be found in English translation in Dan Ben Amos and Jerome R. Mintz, In Praise of the Baal Shem Tov (Bloomington, Ind. 1970), p. 258.

[33]See Noam Elimelech, ed. by Gedaliah Nigal (Jerusalem, 1978), vol. 1, fols. 2b-2c (pp. 10-11) and Nathan of Nemirov, Shivhei ha-Ran (Jerusalem, 1961), p. 17. On the latter, see Arthur Green, Tormented Master (University of Alabama, 1979), p. 55.

[34]In the Megalleh Temirin (Vienna, 1819), two of the subplots involve Hasidim committing acts of seduction and adultery., On Perl's view of Hasidic theology, see Uiber das Wesen der Sekte Chassidim, ed. Abraham Rubinstein (Jerusalem, 1977), pp. 41-43.

[35]Uiber das Wesen, 125 and 146.

[36]"Childhood, Marriage and the Family in the Eastern European Jewish Enlightenment" (forthcoming).

[37]See Aries, Centuries of Childhood and David Gillis, Youth and History (New York, 1974).

[38]Ben-Zion Dinur (ed.), Mikhtavei Avraham Mapu (Jerusalem, 1970), 29 October 1860, p. 133.

[39]For a cogent analysis of Aksenfeld's novel along these lines, see Dan Miron, Ben Hazon le-Emet (Jerusalem, 1979), pp. 177-216.

[40]Baruch Kurzweil, Sifruteinu ha-Hadashah: Hemshekh o-Ma'apekhah? (Tel Aviv, 1971), pp. 234ff.

[41]Introduction to <u>Stempenyu</u> (first published in <u>Yidishe Folks-biblyotek</u> in 1888). <u>Sender Blank</u> is subtitled <u>a roman on a "roman"</u> (a novel without a romance). On this subject, see Dorothy Bilik, "Love in Sholem Aleykhem's Early Novels," Working papers in Yiddish and East European Jewish Studies, n. 10, (YIVO Institute for Jewish Research, 1975).

[42]See Roskies, especially 223-262 and Dan Miron, <u>A Traveler Disguised</u> (New York, 1973), chs. 1 and 2. Roskies is the first to treat seriously the popular literature written in Yiddish.

[43]In addition to Roskies's dissertation cited above, see his annotated bibliography of Dik's writings, <u>The Field of Yiddish</u> (Philadelphia, 1980).

[44]Moses Feivish, <u>Netivot Shalom</u> (Konigsberg, 1858), Sec. 1, para. 2.

[45]Jacob Galis, <u>Encyclopedia Toldot Hakhamei Eretz Yisrael</u> (Jerusalem, 1977), vol. 2, pp. 317-20.

[46]Naphtali Zvi Berlin, <u>He'amek Davar</u> (Vilna, 1879-1880), commentary on Exodus 1:7.

[47]Shaul Stampfer, <u>Shelosh Yeshivot Lita'iot be-Me'ah ha-19</u> (unpublished doctoral dissertation, Hebrew University, 1981), appendix.

[48]Y. M. Epstein, <u>Arukh ha-Shulhan: Even ha-Ezer</u> (Warsaw, 1905-06), Sec. 1, Para. 11:3.

[49]Solomon Mordecai Schwadron, <u>She'elot ve-Tshuvot Mararsham</u> (Warsaw, 1902), Part 1, Q. 195.

[50]Abraham Landau Bornstein, <u>Avnei Nezer</u> (Pieterkov, 1916) Part 1, Q. 119.

[51]Pauline Wengeroff, <u>Memoiren einer Grossmutter</u> (Berlin, 1913), pp. 41-46.

[52]Y. L. Peretz, "Zikhronot" in <u>Kol Kitvei Y. L. Peretz</u> (Tel Aviv, 1957), 146. Even Moses Mendelssohn, despite his claim not to have needed a marriage broker for his own wedding, is said to have taken a <u>shiddukh</u> commission. See Katz, <u>Zion</u>, 50.

[53]Nathan Hurvitz, "Courtship and Arranged Marriages Among Eastern European Jews Prior to World War I as depicted in a <u>Briefenshteller</u>," <u>Journal of Marriage and the Family</u>, (May, 1975): 422-30.

[54]I thank my colleague Elizabeth Fox-Genovese for suggesting this formulation.

NOTES TO "SECULAR RELIGIOSITY"

Mendes-Flohr

[1]For an illuminating discussion of the applicability and limitations of "secularization" as a transcultural category, see R. J. Zwi Werblowsky, <u>Beyond Tradition and Modernity. Changing Religions in a Changing World</u> (London, 1976), pp. 1-20.

[2]Despite the corrosive affects of doubt, an emotional attachment to one's religion may, of course, endure. Rosenzweig tells the story of a Jew who loved the Orthodox service, that is, he passionately enjoyed davening, but when called to read the Torah, the attestation of faith in God and His Torah, he declined because he no longer believed.

[3]Coined by Schleiermacher, the term "religiosity" was systematically developed by the German sociologist Georg Simmel to designate the religious attitude independent of formal, institutional religion. Simmel, however, uses the term in a much broader sense than we, to refer to any attitude of devotion and fidelity be it to politics or stamp collecting. Our use is closer to Schleiermacher's. But whereas he employed "religiosity" to denote the religious emotion per sui, we wish to designate by the term the abiding concern with religious and theological questions independent of one's commitment or lack thereof to a particular religion. For stylistic reasons I shall occasionally refer to secular religiosity as the "modern sensibility," and to the individual of secular religiosity as "the modern individual." I am aware that the modern sensibility and individual can be very far from the concerns we are presently considering.

[4]In fact, in all his massive corpus Schleiermacher makes mention of revelation only once, in a footnote in Der Christliche Glaube (1884 ed., 1, Zustatz) Par. 10, pp. 57-63.

[5]Rosenzweig's analysis of the "ideology of historical theology" is the most incisive that I know. Cf. The Star of Redemption. Trans. W. W. Hallo (New York, 1970), pp. 101-102. In the Jewish context, Krochmal's historiosophical treatise Moreh Nevukhei Ha'Zeman would be a clear exception to this observation.

[6]C. Geertz, Islam Observed (Princeton, 1968), pp. 3, 15.

[7]My argument is not normative; therefore I deliberately say prospect and not danger. In The Heretical Imperative, Peter Berger argues that the process described by Geertz is not only inevitable but salutary. (Cf. my discussion of Berger's thesis in Section IV of this paper, also note 32). Although Berger might find the expression "spiritual solipsism" somewhat extravagant, it is meant only to highlight the process that he himself acknowledges, viz., that in the modern world religious sensibility dislodged from its moorings in an established religion is adrift without a fixed community, and one may wonder, to use Berger's terminology, whether also without a "plausibility structure"?

[8]Cf. "It has been said of nineteenth-century Kulturprotestantismus that what it cultivates is not Protestantism but a pious reverence for Protestantism's past. A similar quip could be made, mutatis mutandis, with reference to modern Judaism. The name of Ahad Ha'am is the first to spring to mind when mention is made of modern, secular 'culture-Judaism,' but that of Mordecai M. Kaplan is no less significant from a sociological point of view. Kaplan's Reconstructionism which considers Judaism as a cultural-social totality is perhaps not a major formative influence, but it is surely a symptomatic expression of much contemporary Jewish life. In fact, it could be argued that much of what is called Judaism both in Israel and in the Diaspora is a series of variations on the Kaplanian theme, often coupled with a

determined effort to dissimulate this fact." Werblowsky, op. cit., p. 50. Charles Liebman makes a similar argument in his detailed study on Reconstructionism. Cf. "Reconstructionism in American Jewish Life," American Jewish Year Book, LXXI (1970), pp. 3-100, esp. 90-97.

[9]When we consider the spiritual leadership appropriate for a post-traditional Jewry it would be well to recall Max Scheler's distinction between Führer and Vorbild, the executive leader who is to be followed through obedience, and the model person who is to be followed through emulation. The Führer, be he a military commander or business executive, issues orders which his subordinates are to obey. The Vorbild embodies paradigmatically values and modes of conduct which serve to inspire emulation. When instrumental objectives are to be attained in the most expedient manner the Führer is manifestly the more appropriate leader; when the objectives are spiritual and require not simply the subordination of the individual's will to a given task but the internalization of ideal values and attitudes, e.g., piety, righteousness and belief, the guide to the attainment of these objectives is the Vorbild. Cf. Max Scheler, "Vorbilder und Führer," Schriften aus dem Nachlass (Berlin 1933). For a masterful summary of Scheler's essay, see Arthur A. Cohen, "The Jewish Intellectual in an Open Society," in Philip Longworth, ed., Confrontations with Judaism (London, 1966), pp. 18-19.

[10]In addition to the talmid chacham, there are of course, other ideal types of individuals, foremostly the zaddik and the hasid. As a Vorbild for classical Judaism, each of the latter types represents, as Scholem observes, "what we would call ethical values, values of the heart and of the deeds of man." The talmid chacham, on the other hand, represents an intellectual-cum-spiritual ideal. He is the ultimate "teacher of his generation," he embodies "the highest aim of education which the Jews have had over the last two thousand years of their history." Gershom Scholem, "Three Types of Jewish Piety," Ariel. Quarterly Review of Arts and Letters in Israel, No. 32, (1973): 9.

[11]Ibid., p. 10.

[12]A. Altmann, "Bildautorität und Wortautorität, Bayerische Israelitische Gemeindezeitung, XII, Jhrg. No. 11 (1 June 1936), p. 244.

[13]Rosenzweig, Briefe (Berlin, 1935), p. 717.

[14]Star of Redemption, pp. 94-97.

[15]Goethe, Faust, part 2, Night.

[16]Cf. Paul Mendes-Flohr and Jehuda Reinharz, "From Relativism to Religious Faith. The Testimony of Franz Rosenzweig's Unpublished Diaries," Leo Baeck Institute Year Book, XII (1977), pp. 161-174.

[17]Star of Redemption, pp. 96 f.

[18]Ibid., p. 97.

[19]Cf. "The Builders: Concerning the Law," in Rosenzweig, On Jewish Learning, ed. by N. N. Glatzer (New York, 1965), pp. 72-92 and 115ff.

[20]Ibid., p. 115. Buber's reply to Rosenzweig is published in On Jewish Learning (see note 19). A passage of a letter only recently published and not appearing in the aforementioned volume, reads: "Offenbarung istnicht Gesetzgebung. Für diesen Satz würde ich in einer jüdischen Weltkirche mit Inquisitionsgewalt hoffentlich zu sterben bereit sein." Buber, Briefwechsel aus sieben Jahrzehnten (Heidelberg, 1973), III, p. 222.

[21]Cf. my "Rosenzweig and Kant. Two Views of Ritual and Religion," in Mystics, Philosophers, and Politicians: Essays in Jewish Intellectual History in Honor of Alexander Altmann, ed. J. Reinharz and D. Swetschinski (Durham, 1981), pp. 315-41.

[22]Buber later discarded this typological distinction between "official" and "subterranean" Judaism as admittedly too contrived and artificial. Although he now recognized the spiritual subtlty of official, normative expressions of Judaism, he nonetheless continued to speak of authentic and inauthentic types of Jewish piety.

[23]For this reason recurrent attempts to establish an "alternative Jewish tradition," such as by Jewish socialists who celebrate the glories of past Jewish revolutionaries and anarchists, will always be sectarian and eventually dissipate.

[24]Cf. Paul Ricoeur, "The 'Sacred' Text and the Community," in W. D. O'Flaherty, ed., The Critical Study of Sacred Text (Berkeley Religious Studies Series, 1979), p. 271.

[25]"On Being a Jewish Person," in Franz Rosenzweig. His Life and Thought, Presented by N. N. Glatzer (New York, 1953), p. 222.

[26]Cf. Briefe, p. 496f. He had hoped to write a comprehensive study of the mitzvoth and their meaning, but, alas, because of his illness he never realized this project.

[27]Eugen Rosenstock-Huessy, ed., Judaism Despite Christianity (New York, 1971), p. 133.

[28]Cf. his essay, "Realpolitik," In his Kleinere Schriften (Berlin, 1935), pp. 409-14.

[29]Cf. A. Altmann, "Franz Rosenzweig on History," in Altmann, ed. Between East and West: Essays dedicated to the Memory of Bela Horovitz (London, 1958), pp. 194-214.

[30]Buber, "Gandhi, Politics, and Us" (1930), in Pointing the Way. Collected Essays. Trans and ed. M. Friedman (New York: 1957), p. 137.

[31]Buber, "Nationalism," Israel and the World. Essays in a Time of Crisis (New York, 1963), p. 225.

[32]P. Berger, The Heretical Imperative: Contemporary Possiblitites of Religious Affirmation (Garden City, 1979), ch. 1.

[33]Ibid., pp. 66-87.

[34]To be sure, in Jerusalem, Mendelssohn acknowledges the Covenant, but only as the Law, or as he put it, "ceremonial laws," which convey universal religious (i.e., metaphysical)

truths in a symbolic fashion and which are to be observed by Israel until some such day that the rest of humankind will free itself from the lure of paganism, anthropomorphism, and the confusion of religion and political power. This "priestly" role as custodians of pristine religious truths exhausts the universal significance of the covenant and Israel's existence as a separate group. The centrality and, indeed, urgency of Israel to the universal process of Heilsgeschichte is thus largely obscured by Mendelssohn. In this context, it should be emphasized that Mendelssohn regarded these religious truths to be rational and thus accessible to all humans independent of Judaism, and of any revealed faith for that matter. This denial of Torah's exclusive claim on truth in effect deprives Judaism of its compelling cognitive force. Thus, it may be said, that Mendelssohn removed Judaism from the province of truth and history.

[35]There is, of course, a logical distinction between "function" and "purpose". The former is epiphenomenal and secondary, the latter is primary, and may or may not be practical in intent.

[36]Many contemporary Orthodox thinkers are more subtle and compelling. Mutatis mutandis, Joseph Soloveitchik and Yeshayahu Leibowitz, for example, argue that heteronomy, or rather theonomy, engenders a meta-empirical reality in which spiritual truths are apprehended.

[37]I follow the apt formulation of Werblowsky, op. cit., p. 49.

NOTES TO "JUDAISM AND MARXISM"

Dobkowski

[1]See Roger Garaudy, From Anathema to Dialogue (London, 1967); Peter Habblethwaite, The Christian-Marxist Dialogue and Beyond (London, 1977); Alexander Miller, The Christian Significance of Marx (London, 1946); José Miranda, Marx Against the Marxists (London, 1980); Miranda, Marx and the Bible (London, 1977); and Gustavo Gutierrez, A Theology of Liberation (London, 1974), as examples.

[2]A cursory look at the published works of some of the most accomplished and significant Jewish scholars, philosophers, historians and sociologists including Y. H. Yerushalmi, Jacob Neusner, Marvin Fox, Arthur A. Cohen, Baruch A. Levine, Michael A. Meyer, Arnold Band, David Blumenthal, Stephen Katz, Lucy Dawidowicz, David Ruderman, Marshall Sklare, Nathan Glazer, Jehuda Reinharz, David Berger, Nahum Sarna, Ruth R. Wisse, Bernard Martin, Richard Rubenstein, etc., to name only a few, should substantiate the point. Those who have focused on the relationship between Judaism and Marxism like Abraham Leon, The Jewish Question: A Marxist Interpretation (New York, 1970), are either polemical in their defense of Marxism or, like Robert Wistrich, ed., The Left Against Zion (London, 1979), Wistrich, Revolutionary Jews from Marx to Trotsky (New York, 1976); Julius Carlebach, Karl Marx and the Radical Critique of Judaism (London, 1978); Solomon Bloom, "Karl Marx and the Jews," Jewish Social Studies, 4:1, pp. 2-16, and Edmund Silberner's important essays on the attitude of socialism toward the Jews,

Hierosolymitana, 7 (Jerusalem, 1956), pp. 778-96, and "Anti-Semitism and Philo-Semitism in the Socialist International," Judaism, 2:2, pp. 121-40, are excessively critical. One refreshing exception is Norman Levine who in a number of articles, particularly his "On the Necessity of a Jewish-Marxist Dialogue" published in Judaism in 1976 has argued for a reasoned discourse between the two traditions with intelligence and insight. I am indebted to his pathbreaking efforts.

[3]Karl Marx, Early Writings (London, 1975), p. 239.

[4]David McLellan, Karl Marx: His Life and Thought (New York, 1973), p. 86.

[5]See Nicholas Lash, A Matter of Hope (Notre Dame, 1982), for a brilliant attempt by a Christian theologian to negotiate an understanding between Christianity and Marxism. I have benefited substantially from his categories and insights.

[6]Richard L. Rubenstein, After Auschwitz (New York, 1966). See Levine, "On the Necessity."

[7]Robert C. Tucker, Philosophy and Myth in Karl Marx (Cambridge, 1972), p. 24.

[8]See Martin Jay, The Dialectical Imagination (London, 1973); Leszek Kolakowski, Main Currents of Marxism, 3 vols. (Oxford, 1978); McLellan, Karl Marx; Tucker, Philosophy and Myth. See also Lash, A Matter of Hope.

[9]Marx, Early Writings, p. 423. See Lash, pp. 36-42.

[10]Karl Marx, Frederick Engels, Collected Works, V (London, 1976), p. 23. See Lash, pp. 40-44.

[11]Ibid.,p. 31. See Lash pp. 64-72.

[12]Marx, Early Writings, pp. 425-26. In the history of human thought there are few texts that have aroused such disagreement, controversy and conflicts of interpretation as this one.

[13]"Preface" to "A Contribution to the Critique of Political Economy", Early Works, p. 426. See Lash, pp. 250-6.

[14]Early Works, p. 27.

[15]See Eric Fromm, ed., Marx's Concept of Man (New York, 1964).

[16]I am indebted to Yochanan Muffs for many of these conceptual insights.

[17]Babylonian Talmud, Sanhedrin 38.

[18]Midrash Tanhuma, Genesis, 7 and following.

[19]See Speiser's translation of the Gilgamesh Epic, in Pritchard, Ancient Near Eastern Texts, 2nd edition, p. 71ff.

[20]Karl Marx, Grundrisse (London, 1973), p. 490.

[21]Abraham Isaac Kook, The Lights of Penitence, The Moral Principles, Lights of Holiness, Essays, Letters, and Poems, Ben Zion Bokser, transl. (New York, 1978), p. 26.

[22]See Hans Kohn, "The Jew Enters Western Culture," Menorah Journal, (April, 1930); Jacob B. Agus, Guideposts in Modern Judaism (New York, 1954); Agus, Modern Philosophies of Judaism (New York, 1941); Nathan Rotenstreich, Tradition and Reality: the Impact of History on Modern Jewish Thought (Washington, D.C., 1961); Kurt Wilhelm, "The Jewish Community in the Post-Emancipation Period," Leo Baeck Institute Yearbook, 2, (1957), pp. 47-75; Alexander Altmann, "Theology in Twentieth-Century German Jewry," Leo Baeck Institute Yearbook, 1, (1956), pp. 193-216. See Levine, "On the Necessity."

[23]See Franz Rosenzweig, The Star of Redemption (New York, 1971); Nahum Glatzer, ed., Franz Rosenzweig: His Life and Thought (New York, 1953). See Levine, "On the Necessity."

[24]Franz Rosenzweig, On Jewish Learning (New York, 1955). See Levine, "On the Necessity."

[25]See Gershom Scholem, From Berlin to Jerusalem (New York, 1980); Scholem, Walter Benjamin: The Story of a Friendship (Philadelphia, 1981); David Biale, Gershom Scholem: Kabbalah and Counter-History (Cambridge, Mass., 1979).

[26]See Walter Benjamin, Illuminations (New York, 1968); Benjamin, Reflections (New York, 1978). See Biale, Gershon Scholem.

[27]See Gershom Scholem, Major Trends in Jewish Mysticism (New York, 1961); Scholem, The Messianic Idea in Judaism (New York, 1971). See Biale, Gershom Scholem.

[28]For a good overview of Lurianic Kabbalism see David Blumenthal, Understanding Jewish Mysticism, (New York, 1978).

[29]Martin Buber, I and Thou (New York, 1970). See Levine, "On the Necessity."

[30]See Buber, Tales of the Hasidim (New York, 1947-1948), as an example. See Levine, "On the Necessity."

[31]Buber, The Prophetic Faith (New York, 1960).

[32]Buber, The Eclipse of God (New York, 1957).

[33]Buber, Israel and the World (New York, 1965). See Levine, "On the Necessity."

NOTES TO "CHURCH-SECT THEORY"

Ellenson

This article is a revision of an address originally delivered at the annual meeting of the Society for the Scientific Study of Religion in Baltimore, Maryland, on November 1, 1981. Several colleagues offered comments at the meeting. I acknowledge with thanks their helpfulness. I would also like to extend a special thanks to my colleague here at HUC-JIR, Stanley

Chyet, for his reading and discussing an earlier version of this paper with me.

[1]Peter Berger, The Sacred Canopy (Garden City, NY, 1967), p. 107.

[2] Ibid., p. 106.

[3]Arnold Eisen, "The Uses of Social Theory in the Study of Modern Judaism," in Baruch Bokser, ed., History of Judaism—The Next Ten Years (Chico, Ca., 1980), p. 129.

[4]On this point, see David Ellenson, "Rabbi Esriel Hildesheimer and the Quest for Religious Authority: The Earliest Years," Modern Judaism, (December, 1981), pp. 279-97.

[5]Ibid.

[6]Charles Liebman, "Orthodoxy in American Jewish Life," in Marshall Sklare, ed., The Jewish Community in America (New York, 1974), pp. 135-36.

[7]Benton Johnson, "On Church and Sect," American Sociological Review, (August, 1963): 541.

[8]Stephen Steinberg, "Reform Judaism: The Origin and Evolution of a 'Church Movement,'" Journal for the Scientific Study of Religion, (October, 1965): 118.

[9]Liebman, "Orthodoxy in American Jewish Life," p. 136.

[10]Johnson, "On Church and Sect," p. 541.

[11]Steinberg, "Reform Judaism," p. 118.

[12]H. Richard Niebuhr, The Social Sources of Denominationalism (Hamden, Ct., 1929).

[13]Liston Pope, Millhands and Preachers (New Haven, 1942).

[14]J. Milton Yinger, Religion in the Struggle for Power (Durham, N.C., 1961).

[15]Bryan Wilson, Sects and Society (Berkeley, 1961).

[16]Rodney Stark and William Brainbridge, "Of Churches, Sects, and Cults: Preliminary Concepts for a Theory of Religious Movements," Journal for the Scientific Study of Religion, (June, 1979): 118.

[17]Ibid.

[18]For an excellent historical summary of the origins of and developments in this theory, see the fine piece by William H. Swatos, Jr., "Weber or Troeltsch? Methodology, Syndrome, and the Development of Church-Sect Theory," Journal for the Scientific Study of Religion, (June, 1976): 129-44.

[19]Liebman, "Orthodoxy," p. 136.

[20]The term "double bind" is mine, but arises from Liebman's discussion (Ibid., pp. 136-37), where he points out the task confronting Jewish religious groups in the modern world is, in fact, four-fold. That is, the Jewish religious group

must meet the group's needs in relation to 1) general society and 2) Jewish society, as well as the individual group member's needs in relation to 3) general society and 4) Jewish society. As this paper is primarily, though not exclusively, concerned with the former rather than the latter set of problems, it seems appropriate to speak of "double bind."

[21]Steinberg, "Reform Judaism," p. 120.

[22]Ibid., p. 117 and p. 125.

[23]Liebman, "Orthodoxy in American Jewish Life," p. 136.

[24]Esriel Hildesheimer, The Responsa of Rabbi Esriel (Tel Aviv, 1969), Orah Hayim, no. 7.

[25]For a summary of this work, see Zvi Benjamin Auerbach, "A Biography of Rabbi Esriel Hildesheimer in His Hometown of Halberstadt," Festschrift for Yehiel Jacob Weinberg (Jerusalem, 1969), p. 235.

[26]The Responsa of Rabbi Esriel, Orah Hayim, no. 7.

[27]Der Orient, (1837), p. 358.

[28]Ibid., pp. 357-60 and 362-64.

[29]Mordecai Eliav. "Rabbi Hildesheimer and His Influence on Hungarian Jewry," (Hebrew) Zion, (1962): 61.

[30]Ibid.

[31]Ibid.

[32]For a description of the Hildesheimer yeshiva and its educational policy, see Mordecai Eliav, "Torah im Derekh Eretz in Hungary," (Hebrew) Sinai, (1962): 127-142.

[33]Cited in Ibid., p. 138.

[34]See Meir Hildesheimer, "Contributions Towards a Portrait of Esriel Hildesheimer," (Hebrew) Sinai, (1964): 76. Other Hungarian rabbis who forbade the use of the vernacular by Jews were Moses Sofer, Responsa of the Hatam Sofer, Hoshen Mishpat, no. 197; Akiba Yoseph Schlesinger, Lev HaIvri, pp. 19a-21b; and Hillel Lichtenstein, Responsa of Bet Hillel, nos. 34, 35, and 39.

[35]Cited in Moredecai Eliav, "Rabbi Hildesheimer and His Influence on Hungarian Jewry," p. 72.

[36]Translated by Alexander Guttmann, The Struggle Over Reform In Rabbinic Literature (Jerusalem and New York, 1977), p. 290.

[37]See Eliav, "Torah im Derekh Eretz in Hungary," pp. 140-141.

[38]For the exchange of letters between Hildesheimer and Assad on this issue, and Hildesheimer's contention that he would write in support of the creation of such a seminary to at least two journals, see Meir Hildesheimer, ed., "Rabbi Judah Assad and Rabbi Esriel Hildesheimer," (Hebrew) Festschrift for Yehiel Jacob Weinberg, pp. 295-297.

[39]Nathaniel Katzburg, "The Jewish Congress of Hungary, 1868-1869," Hungarian Jewish Studies, (1969): 6-7.

[40]Mordecai Eliav, ed., Rabbiner Esriel Hildesheimer Briefe (Jerusalem, 1965), Letter 25 (Hebrew).

[41]On the resolutions of the Mihalowitz Conference and Hildesheimer's view of them, see Esriel Hildesheimer, "Ein Beitrag zur Bedeutung von Chukot HaGoyim," in M. Hildesheimer, ed., Rabbiner Dr. I. Hildesheimer, Gesammelte Aufsätze (Frankfurt, 1923).

[42]Eliav, ed., Hildesheimer Briefe, Letter 22 (Hebrew).

[43]See Nathaniel Katzburg, "The Jewish Congress of Hungary, 1868-1869," pp. 18-19.

[44]Meir Hildesheimer, ed., "Rabbi Judah Assad and Rabbi Esriel Hildesheimer," p. 295.

[45]See Meir Hildesheimer, ed., Gesammelte Aufsätze, p. 57.

[46]See Hildesheimer's essay, "Ueber die Zeugnisufähigkeit der Ubertreter von Religionsgeboten," in Ibid., pp. 36-81, for a full discussion of his views on this issue.

[47]Azriel Hildesheimer, ed., "Rabbi Esriel Hildesheimer on Zacherias Frankel and the Jewish Theological Seminary in Breslau," (Hebrew) HaMaavan (1953): p. 65.

[48]Loew's attacks upon Hildesheimer in the pages of Ben Chananjah appeared throughout the decade (1858-1867) of his editorship.

[49]Meir Hildesheimer, "Contributions Towards A Portrait of Esriel Hildesheimer," p. 78.

[50]Eliav, ed., Hildesheimer Briefe, Letter 20 (Hebrew).

[51]Quoted in Max Sinasohn, ed., Adass Jisroel Berlin: Entstehung, Entfaltung, Entwurzelung, 1869-1939 (Jerusalem, 1966), p. 13.

[52]Ibid., p. 14.

[53]Eliav, ed., Hildesheimer Briefe, Letter 14.

[54]HaMagid (1869), XIII, no. 26.

[55]Meir Hildesheimer, ed., "Writings Regarding the Founding of the Berlin Rabbinical Seminary," (Hebrew) HaMaayan, (1974), p. 14.

[56]Ibid., pp. 29-30.

[57]Eliav, ed., Hildesheimer Briefe, Letter 55.

[58]On this point see Israel Klausner, In The Ways of Zion (Jerusalem, 1978), pp. 149 ff. (Hebrew); and Mordecai Eliav, Love of Zion and the Men of Hod: German Jewry and the Settlement of Eretz-Israel in the 19th Century (Tel Aviv, 1970), p. 405.

[59]See Eliav, ed., Hildesheimer Briefe, Letters 65 and 69 (German) and 35 (Hebrew) for his views on this conference.

[60]Ibid.

[61]Ibid., Letter 69.

[62]Ibid., Letter 29.

[63]Ibid., Letter 86.

[64]Ibid., Letter 68. Also see The Responsa of Rabbi Esriel, Orah Hayim, no. 48; and "Novellae to the Orah Hayim," pp. 123-24, to read of Hildesheimer's concessions to the German environment where Orthodox Jewish children regularly affirmed the worth, and perhaps even superiority, of secular as opposed to Jewish education.

[65]Thus, in his Adass Jisroel congragation the rabbi wore a robe, there was a male choir, and a sermon was delivered in the vernacular. In addition, he continued to wear Western garb and, in his manner and bearing, resembled a German burgher. On this point, see a wonderful contemporary description of Hildesheimer from the viewpoint of a Polish Jew in Jacob Glatstein, Homecoming at Twilight (New York, 1962), pp. 69-71. I am grateful to Professor Steven Zipperstein of Oxford University for bringing this reference to my attention.

[66]Mordecai Eliav, ed., Hildesheimer Briefe, Letters 40 and 78.

[67]Ibid., Letter 61. This concern appears throughout Hildesheimer's works; this letter is just a single example.

[68]Abraham M. Hirsch, "Letters on Palestine From Samuel Montagu to Benjamin Hirsch," Historia Judaica, (1952): 128.

NOTES TO "JEWS AND SOUTHERNERS"

Whitfield

[1]"James Dickey," in George Plimpton, ed., Writers at Work, Fifth Series (New York, 1981), pp. 199, 201, 209, 211-12, 219, 228.

[2]"Joseph Heller," in Ibid., pp. 231, 234-35, 237; Joseph Heller, Catch-22 (New York, 1962), p. 312.

[3]Norman Mailer, The Armies of the Night (New York, 1968), p. 191.

[4]Walker Percy, The Moviegoer (New York, 1967), pp. 88-89.

[5]William Faulkner, Intruder in the Dust (New York, [College Edition] 1948), pp. 194-95.

[6]Stephen S. Wise to A. B. Horwitz, January 19, 1939, in Carl Hermann Voss, ed., Stephen S. Wise: Servant of the People (Philadelphia, 1970), pp. 231-32.

[7]Daniel J. Boorstin, The Americans: The National Experience (New York, 1965), pp. 206-12.

[8]Louis D. Rubin, Jr., The Curious Death of the Novel: Essays in American Literature (Baton Rouge, 1967), p. 131;

Willie Morris, North Toward Home (Boston, 1967), pp. 324-27; Robert Sherrill, The Saturday Night Special (New York, 1973), p. 324; Norman Podhoretz, Breaking Ranks: A Political Memoir (New York, 1979), p. 147.

[9]Irving Howe, World of Our Fathers (New York, 1976), p. 562.

[10]Lionel Trilling, Sincerity and Authenticity (Cambridge, 1972), p. 85; Phillip Knightley, The First Casualty (New York, 1975), p. 320.

[11]Glasgow quoted in Alfred Kazin, On Native Grounds (Garden City, 1956), p. 194; Arthur M. Schlesinger, Jr., A Thousand Days: John F. Kennedy in the White House (Boston, 1965), p. 733; Henry Adams, The Education of Henry Adams (Boston, 1961), pp. 57-58.

[12]Floyd C. Watkins, "The Hound Under the Wagon: Faulkner and the Southern Literati," in Doreen Fowler and Ann J. Abadie, eds., Faulkner and the Southern Renaissance (Jackson, Miss., 1982), p. 113.

[13]Boris Pasternak, Dr. Zhivago (New York, 1958), p. 300; A. Alvarez, Under Pressure: The Writer in Society (Baltimore, 1965), p. 173.

[14]Rubin, Curious Death of the Novel, pp. v, 268-69, 270, 275, 276-77, 279; Irving Howe, ed., Jewish-American Stories (New York, 1977), pp. 4-6.

[15]Delmore Schwartz to Dwight Macdonald, July 25, 1943, in Box 45, Folder 1116, Dwight Macdonald Papers, Yale University.

[16]Morris, North Toward Home, pp. 384-85, 387.

[17]Charles Y. Glock and Rodney Stark, Christian Beliefs and Anti-Semitism (New York, 1966), p. 23; Eli N. Evans, The Provincials: A Personal History of Jews in the South (New York, 1973), pp. 124-39.

[18]Carson McCullers, The Ballad of the Sad Cafe (Boston, 1951), pp. 8, 65; Virginia Spencer Carr, The Lonely Hunter: A Biography of Carson McCullers (Garden City, New York, 1975), pp. 236-38.

[19]Richard Wright, Black Boy: A Record of Childhood and Youth (New York, 1966), pp. 70-71.

[20]Booker T. Washington, Up from Slavery (New York, 1963), pp. 23-24; F. Holton, "John Hope Franklin, Scholar," University of Chicago Magazine, 73 (September 1980): 14.

[21]F. Scott Fitzgerald, The Last Tycoon (New York, 1970), p. 13.

[22]Katherine Anne Porter, "A Country and Some People I Love," Harper's, 231 (September 1965): 68.

[23]"The Editor Interviews William Styron," Modern Occasions, 1 (Fall 1971): 501-2, 510.

[24]Philip Roth, The Professor of Desire (New York, 1978), pp. 129-30.

[25]Howe, Jewish-American Literature, pp. 14-15, and World of Our Fathers, pp. 588-90.

[26]Howe, Jewish-American Literature, p. 3; Isaac Rosenfeld, An Age of Enormity: Life and Writing in the Forties and Fifties (Cleveland, 1962), p. 272.

[27]Simon Rawidowicz, "Israel: The Ever-dying People," in Studies in Jewish Thought (Philadelphia, 1974), p. 211.

[28]Louis Harap, The Image of the Jew in American Literature: From Early Republic to Mass Immigration (Philadelphia, 1974), p. 261; Joseph Blau and Salo W. Baron, eds., Jews of the United States, 1790-1840: A Documentary History (New York, 1963), II, p. 417.

[29]Ezra Goodman, The Fifty-Year Decline and Fall of Hollywood (New York, 1961), pp. 340-43; Lewis S. Feuer, "Spinoza's Thought and Modern Perplexities: Its American Career," in Barry S. Kogan, ed., Spinoza: A Tercentenary Perspective (Cincinnati, 1979), p. 58; Mordecai Richler, Shovelling Trouble (London, 1973), p. 6.

[30]Lillian Hellman, review of Eli N. Evans, The Provincials, New York Times Book Review, November 11, 1973, p. 5.

[31]"Lillian Hellman," in George Plimpton, ed., Writers at Work, Third Series (New York, 1967), p. 121; Lillian Hellman, Pentimento: A Book of Portraits (Boston, 1973), pp. 171-72, 180; Katherine Lederer, Lillian Hellman (Boston, 1979), p. 39.

[32]Lillian Hellman, An Unfinished Woman: A Memoir (New York, 1970), pp. 2-3, 6, 7, 132-34.

[33]Eric F. Bentley, ed., Thirty Years of Treason: Excerpts from Hearings before the House Committee on Un-American Activities, 1938-1968 (New York, 1971), pp. 533, 537.

[34]Lillian Hellman, Scoundrel Time (New York, 1977), pp. 38-39.

[35]Ibid., pp. 39, 43.

[36]Harap, Image of the Jew, p. 192.

[37]William Faulkner, "The Bear," in Three Famous Short Novels (New York, 1961), p. 279; Alfred J. Kutzik, "Faulkner and the Jews," in YIVO Annual of Jewish Social Science, 13 (1965), pp. 213-26.

[38]Elizabeth Nowell, Thomas Wolfe: A Biography (Garden City, 1960), p. 86; Louis D. Rubin, Jr., Thomas Wolfe: The Weather of His Youth (Baton Rouge, 1955), pp. 106-7.

[39]Leo Gurko, Thomas Wolfe: Beyond the Romantic Ego (New York, 1975), pp. 25, 41, 96-97, 118; B. R. McElderry, Jr., Thomas Wolfe (New York, 1964), p. 151.

[40]Richard S. Kennedy, The Window of Memory: The Literary Career of Thomas Wolfe (Chapel Hill, 1962), pp. 88, 329; Nowell, Thomas Wolfe, p. 98.

[41]Flannery O'Connor, The Habit of Being: Letters (New York, 1979), p. 539.

[42]Harper Lee, <u>To Kill a Mockingbird</u> (New York, 1962), pp. 149, 246-50.

[43]William Styron, <u>Sophie's Chice</u> (New York, 1980), pp. 45-46, 196-99.

[44]Walker Percy, <u>The Second Coming</u> (New York, 1980), pp. 7-9, 11-12, 15, 19.

[45]Nelson Algren, <u>A Walk on the Wild Side</u> (New York, 1977), pp. 81, 117.

[46]Mailer, <u>Armies of the Night</u>, pp. 65, 153; Michael Halberstam, <u>The Wanting of Levine</u> (New York, Berkeley, 1979), pp. 171-77, 220.

[47]Philip Roth, <u>The Great American Novel</u> (New York, 1973), p. 267.

[48]Woody Allen, <u>The Nightclub Years, 1964-1968</u> (United Artists).

[49]Jack Temple Kirby, <u>Media-Made Dixie</u> (Baton Rouge, 1978), <u>passim</u>; Eli N. Evans, "Movies Alter the Image of the South," <u>New York Times</u>, May 24, 1981, pp. 17, 22; Ted Sennett, <u>Your Show of Shows</u> (New York, 1977), pp. 54-55; Nichols quoted in <u>This Fabulous Century</u>, 1950-1960 (New York, 1970), p. 227; Tom Lehrer, <u>Too Many Songs</u> (New York, 1981), pp. 24-27.

NOTES TO "ARTSCROLL"

Levy

[1]Issued by Masorah Publications, the series now contains five volumes on Genesis, three on Ezekiel, five on Psalms, and single volumes on Jonah, Joshua, Daniel and each of the five Scrolls. The beginning of the <u>History of the Jewish People: The Second Temple Period</u> is also devoted to the Biblical period. Eighteen volumes of the commentary were published between 1976 and 1980, while (as far as I am able to determine from the volumes available in Montreal) only three appeared between 1981 and 1982.

[2]Cf. B. Barry Levy, "Judge Not A Book By Its Cover," <u>Tradition</u>, 19:1 (Spring 1981), the letter to the editor by Emanuel Feldman in 19:2, and the accompanying editorial note.

[3]See Artscroll to Ruth, p. xxix, <u>Bereishis</u>, pp. 265, 327, 472, 708, etc. and Jonah 2:4. Inclusion of these sources and reliance on Berosus have been discussed in "Our Torah, Your Torah and Their Torah: An Evaluation of the Artscroll Phenomenon" pp. 146-147 and the article listed in note 2, pp. 91-92. The former study, completed in May of 1979, has been published in <u>Truth and Compassion: Essays on Judaism and Religion in Memory of Rabbi Dr. Solomon Frank</u>, edited by H. Joseph J. Lightstone and M. Oppenheim, (Waterloo, 1982), but has circulated widely since its completion. The latter is a brief presentation of its more salient points.

[4]"Our Torah, Your Torah and Their Torah," pp. 147-162.

[5]Aside from M. Segal's 130 page Hebrew book <u>Parshanut HaMiqra'</u>, itself inadequate and long out of date, there is no book length study on the history of Jewish Biblical interpretation. There are books on specific periods or schools of interpretation and important studies on all sorts of specific issues, periods, and commentators, but there is no work that brings Jubilees, the Zohar, Ibn Ezra, Yefet ben Ali, the Malbim, Philo and the Netsiv together and relates them as exegetes. The three volume <u>Cambridge History of the Bible</u> has covered Jewish interpretation in a very inadequate way, and Smalley's <u>The Study of The Bible in The Middle Ages</u> is similarly limited. I hope to correct this situation as soon as possible.

Hermeneutical literature is even more limited, for the lists of 7, 13, 32 and 49 <u>middot</u> are hardly a literature. The most extensive text of this sort is the Malbim's 613 rules called <u>Ayyellet HaShachar</u> and published as the introduction to his commentary on Leviticus.

[6]The only thing that comes close is the brief Hebrew statement in the first volume on Genesis, discussed below. Judging from the lack of a systematic presentation, it may be somewhat hasty to assume that Artscroll actually has a hermeneutical program at all. Different rabbis have been designated to cull comments about Biblical matters from a host of secondary sources and their individual attitudes -- or those of the editors -- have shaped the series. A clear interpretative program, while no small task, would clarify for everyone -- including the various Artscroll writers -- exactly what Artscroll is trying to do. There are, however, some observable patterns in the volumes that allow for the generalizations about its attitudes and approaches.

[7]Cf. the introductions of Ibn Ezra, Nachmanides and Epstein (<u>Torah Temimah</u>) to their commentaries on the Torah; Abarbanel's introduction to his commentary on the former Prophets; Rashban to Gen. 37:1, etc.

[8]Thus, for example, Psalm 137 "By The Rivers of Babylon" is presented by Artscroll as Davidic, following Gittin 57b. Song of Songs Rabbah 4:1 lists Ezra among the contributors to the Psalms, allowing a post-Davidic date for part of the book, but no reference to this text has been included here. Attitudes of several medieval writers who dealt with this issue have been discussed in Uriel Simon's Hebrew book <u>Four Approaches to the Book of Psalms: From Saadya Gaon to Abraham Ibn Ezra</u>, (Ramat Gan, 1982). Ibn Chiquitilla, an approved Artscroll source (cf. below note 37), dated Psalm 137 to exilic times, and comments by Ibn Ezra and Radak are ambiguous enough to allow this position also, but it has been ignored.

[9]I have discussed this more fully in "Our Torah, Your Torah and Their Torah," note 81. See, more recently, the discussion of the history of parallelism contained in James Kugel, <u>The Idea of Biblical Poetry: Parallelism and its History</u> (New Haven, 1981).

[10]This attitude pervades his introductions and commentaries on poetic passages and books.

[11]This undated letter may be a reaction to the conclusion drawn in "Our Torah, Your Torah and Their Torah," that Feinstein supported Artscroll as an anthology but not a commentary. Other changes that may be responses to criticisms discussed there and

in "Judge Not A Book By Its Cover" include a more careful use of the term Haskamah ("Approbation") with reference to the letters of greetings published in many volumes and the elimination of the bibliographies, on which see further, note 37, below.

[12]See note 4, above.

[13]To some extent this principle has been developed by Maimonides, but his sources were late. Perhaps he assumed the antiquity of medieval pagan practices, which might then be compared to similarly ancient Jewish ones. The principle enunciated in the Guide (III, 50) is most important, however: "Just as . . . the doctrines of the Sabians are remote from us today, the chronicles of those times are likewise hidden from us today. Hence if we knew them and were cognizant of the events that happened in those days, we would know in detail the reasons of many things mentioned in the Torah." (Translation of Pines, p. 615.)

[14]An interesting example is the story of Sennacherib's seige of Jerusalem in the eighth century BCE, related in Isaiah, Kings and Chronicles. The availability of Sennacherib's own annals should theoretically have answered many questions and has, but whether he beseiged the city once or twice still remains a scholarly problem (for detalis see John Bright, A History of Israel, 2nd edition, (Philadelphia, 1972), pp. 296-308). What seems to have gone unnoticed is that the one invasion - two invasion problem was anticipated by Radak and Abarbanel, and no one has really improved on their observations very much, though new facts, theories and conjectures have clarified other aspects of the subject.

[15]This should not be taken as a claim that archaeology or modern scholarship offers no challenge to the accuracy of any Biblical text; far from it. While the availability of new materials often confirms what was not accepted previously, it often poses new problems as well. But in which period of Jewish intellectual history was there no challenge from new modes of thought or sources of information? The challenges of modern discovery may be more solid than earlier philosophical ones, but the latter were probably taken more seriously by Jewish religious writers.

[16]Modern Jewish scholars who have used the classical writers to great advantage include B. Ehrlich, Mikra KiPheshuto; Umberto Cassuto, commentaries to Genesis, Exodus; Moshe Held in a series of articles; Moshe Greenberg, Understanding Exodus; and others who have consciously endeavored to build a modern Jewish approach on the contributions of earlier writers. Non-Jewish recognition of this area is less frequent, but see B. Childs, Exodus (an excellent example); M. Pope, Song of Songs (Anchor Bible), etc.

[17]There is an important attack on the Documentary Hypothesis that has been completely ignored: David Hoffman's Die wichtigsten Instanzen gegen die Graf-Wellhausensche Hypothese, originally published in 1904 and translated into Hebrew under the title Ra'ayot Makhriyot Neged Wellhausen. Hoffman's other works are cited frequently. Had Artscroll been prepared to admit being engaged by contemporary problems, it might have referred to this work also.

[18]I appreciate the fears of those contemporary writers who oppose the use of "critical" editions and new texts that have

not been part of the traditional yeshiva education, but this is not justifiable. After all, Hebrew manuscripts have values other than providing aesthetically pleasing dustjackets.

These attractive illuminations are not without their own message, though. The bucolic scene of David playing his lyre while surrounded by animals (on the dustjackets of Tehillim) is a case in point. This was a very popular manner in which this king was portrayed by artists over the centuries, but many art historians have interpreted such pictures as a transfer to the Biblical David of the characteristics of Orpheus, son of Apollo, who charmed the wild beasts by playing on his lyre! It is indeed strange for Artscroll to have chosen this portrayal of David for the covers of several of its volumes.

[19]Maimonides: Guide, III, 29, 37, etc., Sefer HaMitzvot, Negative Commandments 42; Nachmanides: Introduction to Commentary on the Torah, end of Commentary on the Torah; Abarbanel: See the sources cited in M. S. Segal's collected studies entitled Massoret uBiqqoret, Jerusalem: n.d., pp. 255-257; Chajes: Mavo' HaTalmud, end of chapter 18 (English translation, pp. 152-3), etc. Interesting for comparison is Maimonides, Ibid., 10.

While spokesmen of more open approaches were not lacking, frequently their works had to be defended from attacks (real or anticipated) from innocent, ignorant, or foolish critics. One less known apologia of this type is found in the conclusion of Ibn Aknin's commentary on The Song of Songs (pp. 490 ff.), a work cited and approved by Artscroll. After admitting that his reputation might deter otherwise zealous antagonists from accusing him of heresy, Ibn Aknin outlined how some of his methods really derived from Chazal: Comparative philology derives from the rabbis' use of Greek and various Semitic and non-Semitic languages to explain many Biblical words. (Cf. The introduction to Ibn Janach's Sefer HaRiqma for an earlier text arguing the same point.) Rav Hai, it is noted, used not only Arabic words but also love poetry, the Koran, and the Hadith for comparative purposes. Saadiah did likewise even earlier, in fulfillment of the rabbinic teaching "Anyone who states something wise, even if he be non-Jewish, is called a wise man and one is obligated to transmit it" (Megilla 16a). Rav Hai, it was reported, even wanted to consult the local Catholics on the meaning of a verse in Psalms. When his messenger to the churchman hesitated, he reprimanded him, noting that the earlier authorities consulted members of other religions for linguistic information. It is not clear from this version of the story if the messenger or Hai himself then met the Christian leader, but the desired information was obtained and recorded.

[20]Russel J. Hendel, "Towards a Definition of Torah," Proceedings of the Association of Orthodox Jewish Scientists, Vol. III -IV (1976).

[21]Ibid., p. 183.

[22]I have followed the text of J. I. Gorfinkle's edition, The Eight chapters of Maimonides on Ethics (New York, 1912) but the translation of this passage has been modified.

[23]Cf. the description of the stars as God's "emissaries to preside over the natural functioning of the universe" (Bereishis, p. 600).

²⁴The matter is discussed in The Journal of The American Medical Association, Vol. 238: 15 and 16. The quotation is from Vol. 240, No. 2: 100.

²⁵Cf. the various essays in A. Carmell and C. Domb (ed.) Challenge: Torah Views on Science and Its Problems (London, 1976).

²⁶Modern analyses of the creation and flood narratives by geologists and by historians of religion differ greatly. What scholars of Science may declare impossible or errors, scholars of the Humanities actually perceive as important religious advancements. Is there no way for Orthodox thought to accomodate itself to these different approaches?

²⁷Benedict de Spinoza, A Theologico-Political Treatise, Chapter 7.

²⁸But see the beginning of chapter 8, Ibid.

²⁹See, for example, Nachmanides on Genesis 18:1 and Maimonides' opinion, cited there and analyzed. Also of note are various sections of Joseph Sarachek, Faith and Reason: The Conflict over the Rationalism of Maimonides (New York, 1935).

³⁰Of course I do not assume that the reconstructed history will be identical to the simple meaning of the Biblical text, but that must be the jumping off point.

³¹On the history of rabbinic attitudes towards midrash and aggadah, see now the first chapter of Marc Saperstein's Decoding The Rabbis: A Thirteenth-Century Commentary on The Aggadah (Cambridge, Mass: 1980). The emotional reactions that challenges to midrash still stimulate are exemplified by Fabian Schonfeld's letter in Tradition, 20:1. See also the response scheduled to appear in 20:4.

³²Chajes' attitudes pervade many of his writings, but a most important text is his Mavo' HaTalmud, available in English under the Title The Student's Guide Through The Talmud (New York, 1960). The second part of this work, chapters 17-32, represents one of the most important breakthroughs of any recent writer on the religious position regarding the development, methods and authority of midrash and aggadah.

³³S. Greeneman (ed.) Collected Letters of The Hazon Ish (Hebrew) Vol. I, No. 15: 42.

³⁴How to Teach Torah (Lakewoood, N.J.: 1972), pp. 3-4.

³⁵Cf. the analysis of G. Scholem, On the Kabbalah and its Symbolism, chapter 3, "Kabalah and Myth," (New York, 1965).

³⁶Ibid., p. 33.

³⁷The early volumes contain annotated bibliographies, but, as I have demonstrated elsewhere, they borrow some sentences from The Encyclopaedia Judaica (without due credit) and contain a number of errors. Artscroll's response to this criticism has been to drop the bibliographies altogether. Thus Joshua and the last volumes of Genesis and Psalms lack this important section. As unfortunate as these shortcomings may be, the bibliographies are essential. How many readers can identify the Rabbi Moshe cited in Psalm 122:1 as Ibn Chiquitilla? The reference has

crept in via Ibn Ezra -- as happened with the Karaite Yefet ben Ali in Yonah. Does this mean that Ibn Chiquitilla is also an approved source? Besides, which non-specialist will be able to identify Chazah Zion, Minchas Shai, Ibn Yachya, HaYitzhari, Midrash Halsamari, R. Azaryah Figo, etc? Has Artscroll decided once and for all that the identity of a commentator is irrelevant to one's understanding his interpretations?

[38]See, for example, the letters to the editor of Tradition published in 19:2, 19:4 and 20:4. Thanks are due to Professor Jacob Neusner for requesting this article and to Mr. Joel Linsider for his assistance in proofreading.